Gerard Gardens 1967 to 1978

From the Cradle to the Giant's Grave

By

Bobby Parry

*Cover portrait by Gerard Fleming, who resided at
25d Gerard Gardens.
Cover sketch by Joe O 'Connell who also lived in
23c Gerard Crescent.*

*All of the stories are from my own recollections and
should be viewed with an open mind.*

First published 2010 by Countyvise Ltd,
14 Appin Road, Birkenhead, CH41 9HH

British Library Cataloguing in Publication Data.
A catalogue record for this book is available from the British Library.

ISBN 978 1 906823 44 3

Foreword

by
Dr Frank Carlyle

When people start to recall the days of living in their old neighbourhoods, the nostalgia floods back at a canter as to whether they would be fond memories or otherwise! I can personally remember the days of growing up in both Gerard Gardens and Gerard Crescent with a glowing fondness for both of these fabulous emporiums. I recall these times with much affection as we shared some wonderful times together. Maybe that would be from going to school or on to our many days out at the seaside where we would really know how to have a good time. We would make up our own fun, as the children of our time inevitably had to do but that just added to the excitement. Who can forget going to Ainsdale or to New Brighton on the ferry armed with just jam butties and a bottle of tap water to see us through the hot sweltering days ahead. There were no computers or i pods about in these tough times and I also recall there being no televisions in our small bedrooms. We grew up and slept in these great gardens with some kind of fun or escapade never too far away. The lads would amuse themselves by maybe playing a game of rounders with the girls or more invitingly, a game football with the boys (aaaaah! those were the days my friends) and I hasten to remember that the girls always seemed to win. Why was that?

However, when you look back at our childhood and us growing up into young adults then we do tend to forget about some of these great memories which can be a bit of a shame really. We should dwell on these cherished times of happiness and do all we can to keep such great memories alive. The older you become then the easier it is for your memories to cloud over and almost disappear without a trace into the back of your mind. Names start to become a blur as do some of the incidents that would occur in the neighbourhood or maybe even at school and these memories would lay in the confines for a very long time indeed. Someone once said to me "wouldn't it be great to have a time machine so we could travel back in time"? Well Gerard Gardens old boy Bobby Parry has not got a time machine but he has got the next best thing and that is his fascinating and nostalgic memories of this great place. People from all walks of life would all aspire to this great setting at one time or another and it will never ever be forgotten. Bobby has written this wonderful autobiography that is cleverly titled "From the cradle to the giant's grave" and it is an amazing insight into the happy times that he spent there.

This recollection of memories is a must read for all of the old inhabitants of the squares and I will guarantee you that people who scrutinise this book will be saying, "I remember them", or, "Oh I remember that." Some of the memories and incidents that were a total blur to me have now been re-mastered for me to marvel at and it is all down to this book and Bobby's own encapsulating version of a time machine! Well done lad, from another old boy who himself is also very proud to have been born and bred in the safe confines of Gerard Gardens!

Introduction

by
Bobby Parry

I originally started writing this book on 1st July 2006 which was also my son Jay's 9th birthday. I left my notes to gather dust for years until I found them again and so my amazing journey would begin. Life goes on I suppose and this book will undoubtedly help me to move on to bigger and better things for which I strive for every day. Hopefully one day I will achieve my trusted aims and I will use this book as a platform to further such aspirations. Rather than referring to my old notes, I have decided to start all over again because I do not want any part of this book to be scripted away on some false dawn. I can be a little bit more forthright with my views now because my lovely mother has sadly passed away and I know that she is with me forever and guiding me to express myself as the child that I was in Gerard Gardens. This is my tribute to her and I hope that I have done her proud with my intimate revelations of a happy childhood. Please understand that this is my version of events only and all content is to the best of my wayward knowledge. Incidents may seem exaggerated a little but give me a child who does not elaborate and I will say what-evvvvvvvvvvvvvvvver! I have used linguistic terms in this book that some people will not understand but I have done this for a reason. It is to make people ask my generation questions about what these basic terms mean and so it creates topics of discussion. This will give people more of an understanding of what the scene at the time was all about and hopefully it will be seen as a clever ploy on my behalf.

Being born in Gerard Gardens can only be described as a gift from god for me and I do not say that lightly for fear of being struck down by Father Baker. He was our parish priest for years and one of the many legends that existed in my era and who I will mention further on in this book of notable legends. My aim is to resurrect all that I put before you and to warm the cockles of your heart with pure nostalgia. A bit over the top you might think but this great place deserves to be spoken about in these words of pure adulation. You will know where I am coming from because it is engrained on every single person's soul who would be lucky enough to share all of the many magical moments that I experienced as a kid. It will be resurrected back to life for you as I set out on my own epic adventure trail and I have not got a clue as to where this trail will disembark. Every word will be greeted with my own special twist on it to make this story flow with entertainment as you are transported back to the hippy movement days of my birthplace.

These tenements were so great and a massive privilege to be part of as my testimony will reveal in great depth. I will give you the complete social scene and the very fabric of a community that is still revered today and I will try to live out my own personal experiences. This blessed community will live on forevermore within books like this and I really hope that my work is spot on as a debutant author. My effort has been proof read by my friend and fellow 'Gardenite', Annmarie Welch and also my brother Franky who both shared these adventures with me and they have both given it a 'massive' thumb of approval. In turn their views have given me the confidence to get this little gem published and I thank them for that because it is really important for me to get it right. Our Franky has also guided me on this book and he has given me plenty of food for thought as to what I can safely get away with without the risk of offending anyone. This is the last thing that I would ever want to do and I have been pretty careful with my portrayal but I have also taken a bit of a gamble. I have taken on board his views and done so with so much care and consideration for both my readers and more importantly my loving family. My relief is apparent thanks to his intervention and although it was very painful for me to do I have re scripted a miniscule amount of this book in order to keep the happy medium flowing. I am definitely feeling a Gardens revival at the moment and with your help we can all keep this fabulous place firmly on the map. Thank you to everyone who has given me the drive and the much needed support to share with you all of my very happy childhood memories. I will now embark on my solitary endeavours in this little theme park of life's lost innocence and I will achieve my mission with the help of my literate legions.

I will also mention the other famous landmarks in our midst but I cannot dwell on these communities because I did not live there. These great tenements yielded a spirit that was likened to ours because the people were cast from the same mould. Vauxhall, Fontenoy and Portland Gardens were just a few to name and they added to the magic of our area with their own history and intrigue. I would hang around this celebrated area from time to time but spent most of my time in the epicentre of Gerard Gardens itself. Other tenements in the proximity included St Andrews Gardens which was known as the "Bullring" and of course the "Four Squares". The "Bullring" is still proudly standing and I often take my own 2 kids up there to marvel at this empire of great architecture. These sound communities also displayed their own greatness and my views on these communities are that of the child that I was at the time. Their greatness can only be told by the people who lived there and my only memories of the four squares are littered with battles. Please understand that I have used a lot of banter in this book and my reflections on other tenement blocks are exactly that. Although we fought a lot, these tenements were also great places to live in and had their own legendary status respectively.

I ask everyone to read this book with an open mind because my only intention is to give you all a good read and a little bit of innocent adulation. Incidents that I recall are just written in the way that I remember them and I honestly want to portray that innocence to all of you. There is also rivalry in this book relating to the Orange Lodge Order and the troubles that we both shared at the time. Just chill out and remember that this book is a comic portrayal of a young lad who was caught up in the magical era of the 1970's. I could not have written this book without all of these great institutions and my immense thanks are offered to them all for the many scraps that were often incurred in the name of Status quo!

I feel totally blessed coming from a community that so thrived in the 1970's and that was also evident in the many years before my time. It was a passage of time that still lives and breathes with me to this very day and I still get belly flips every time our name is mentioned. Everywhere I go I still carry a piece of Gerard Gardens with me because I will never let it be banished to the less informative history books. I will carry my passion forward with me until the day that I die because my memories will never ever cease to exist but they need to be documented. This is why I decided to write this book and that decision coincided with the sad passing of my beloved mother 'Patricia (shields) Parry'. My book is a tribute to her and the many other people from my family who left their own indelible mark on me and gave me the tools that I needed to illustrate this tall story.

In order to follow the contents of this book I must ask you to read it through the eyes of a child otherwise you may get lost. I am sure that I will rekindle many of your own happy memories of this magical and enterprising place but you will have to help me by completely cutting off and instilling a clear mind. I have simplified my story as the child that I was so that you can read it to your kids and them to their kids. This will keep our dreams alive and the happy cycle will continue in all of them and all because of where YOU were born. So here we go folks as I take on the mammoth task of engrossing and captivating all of your hearts and souls. I have all the weapons that I need for this job but the main weapon is of course me and my shield is my conscience. All of my stories are spoken with the words and beliefs of a child and that child will reveal himself before your very eyes. If my accounts appear to be farfetched or exaggerated then this only adds to the magic of being back there because that's what kids will always do and that's why we all love them so much!

From the Cradle to the Giant's Grave

The foundation stone of Gerard Gardens was laid on the 21st June 1935 by Sir Kingsley Wood who was the Minister for Health at the time. A massive but much needed project was implemented as part of a programme to rid the city centre of the depressing slums and their deplorable hygiene issues. These problems brought the city dwellers to their knees as they struggled in filth and poverty on an everyday basis that was both demoralising and also so life threatening. The vast tenements were modelled on a similar project in Europe that was known as The 'Karl Marx Hoff' tenements and they were absolutely breathtaking. These blocks were built in Vienna and served as a template to Liverpool's massive building programme that was to change the face of the city centre forever. The construction of Gerard Gardens was overseen by a man named Lancelot Keay, who considered this very project as the one closest to his heart and he was knighted in 1947 for his outstanding work as a public servant. Gerard Street and the surrounding slums were transformed into vast concrete blocks with all the amenities on show that were much needed to help the great communities to both survive and then to ultimately prosper.

Amongst this invigorated community, there existed a brand of people who brought so much to our shores in both their industry and also their own culinary expertise. This was of course The Italian folk who left their own homes to escape the ravages of war and in time they became an integral part of everything that was great about theirs and our new homeland. They would join the massive influx of Irish settlers who came here after the potato famine had left most of Ireland ravaged and together they prospered underneath one unique banner which was of course Catholicism! This vast area was known as 'Little Italy' and many of the settlers went on to marry into the community which of course gave us the very heartbeat of Gerard Gardens itself. Times were not always great though and it took the people of the community a while to adjust to each other but the catholic faith brought everyone together as one. We have to thank God for this hand of fate that produced hundreds of amazing families in our very cosmopolitan midst of inhabitants. Relationships were formed and the people from the very different backgrounds and cultures became united as they mingled with each other. They raised their own families up along the way and it was not long before the solid core of the community prevailed. We may have varied origins to our heritage but one thing for sure is our pedigree as the true and original Scousers of this earth. For that reason amongst others, I am "beat your chest" proud to be known as a 'Gardenite' and I thank everybody from every nation who contributed so willingly in making our happy and massive commune, a national treasure!

The residents were now incorporating a sense of pride and notability as the gleeful dwellers of such luxury and on their very own doorstep. The bad times were good for a change and the bond just grew and grew into a mass of happy gatherings that was being played out on every single landing. At last they had the security to raise their oversized families together albeit safe in the knowledge that their offspring could enjoy all the trappings of this vast playground. This habitual garden was so beautifully presented to the residents with jaw dropping splendour and grandiose on a scale that was never seen before on these historical shores. Mothers could do whatever came naturally to them on the many landings of these fabulous homes and part of that scene would become a jangling paradise. A community soon emerged and these well heeled people prospered on what was to become the legend of Gerard Gardens itself. It went from a pipe dream, to a stark reality and this was where my dreams were born and will now begin in pandemonium!

I was actually born in 7b Gerard Gardens on April 22nd 1967 and was delivered by my grandmother who was known as the wonderful 'Nellie Shields'. I was also helped into this world by her then lifelong friend the great 'Jane (golden) Goulding' who is also a lovely woman.

I still see Jane from time to time and I always remind her of her home made marmalade that I loved so much and she is truly marvellous for her age, as is her marmalade. Nellie was my mother's mam and she was married to Joseph Shields who was my grandfather. Unfortunately I never had the chance to meet my grandfather because he died before I was born and I felt a little bit ripped off by this fact. 7b was their original address and they raised their own family here until my widowed nana moved round to 23b Gerard Crescent. My own mum and dad moved into this humble abode to start a new life having lived in Fitzclarence Street in the early part of their marriage. Together they set up home in the more than comfortable surroundings of what was now our flat and we were well on our way to happiness. My dad Francis Parry met and fell in love with my mother and they married in St. Josephs church on July 11th 1964. My mother was pregnant with my older brother Franky at the time who himself entered the world on 13th December 1964 and was closely followed by my sister Lorraine. She announced herself to the world on 8th February 1966 which was the day after my own mother's 22nd birthday and with them being so close together, I often got their birthdays mixed up.

As you can probably work out, it was obvious that we did not have a television set in the early days but as time went by, we had everything that was required to make us really happy. We were so content within our quaint little home and life was fine and dandy in our very safe environment. My father's parents and my grandparents were my namesake Robert Parry and Sarah Joyce who along with my mother's parents went on to live in the adjoining tenement blocks known as Gerard Crescent! This was as much a feature as the Gardens itself and their residents helped us in exactly the same way that all of our great neighbours seemed to do for each other at this time. Gerard Crescent also incorporated Cartwright, Lionel, Downe, and Thurlow House respectively and the residents were part of the massive infrastructure. The magnitude of the place was immense and the spirit of this special community saw them through the devastating bomb raids by The Luftwaffe in the Second World War. These pioneers of unity survived countless other extremities that would literally batter them as they sheltered in their homes and held on for their dear lives. They were the downtrodden few who would not submit to anything and ultimately this fact would make them the chief architects of our greatness! The unique fabric that we possess in each and every one of us today has been richly entwined into our hearts forever and it's this special fondness that made me want to write this book in the first place.

Going back to the 1940's and my need to express to you the many facts about the devastating impact that the war would have on the many residents of this city centre complex. The constant pummelling that Hitler's men dished out on a regular and prolonged basis saw the residents bombed out of their houses and into the many air raid shelters that were dotted about this vast enemy target. Many families actually hid under their coffee tables when the raids started and believe it or not but these little wooden constructions saved many lives. A great loss of life was reported and the city centre was left in bits by the despicable Nazi's and their even nastier regime. On one devastating occasion 200 people lost their lives when a 'Gerry bomb' was dropped directly on to an air raid shelter in Blackstock Gardens. A lot of the people who perished on that dreadful day had been on a tram and it really did shake the foundations of the under siege and very frightened residents. The raids started in 1940 and continued for 2 years with the loss of 4000 people within the city centre alone and it was at its height in May 1941. Hundreds of buildings were destroyed in this campaign of terror and lives were literally turned upside down as the area was decimated on a large scale. For the people of this community, it was a coming together as to speak and the start of a very long love affair which still prevails today in such angst and invigorating warmth. People dusted themselves down and put the horrors of war behind them to establish a community that was unseen or unheard of in any other walk of life. Together they forged ahead and fought back with great dignity and an abundance of pride. This dream just rolled on in the face of adversity and went forward at a very quick pace as the people would hurriedly put their lives back together again. The thriving district was a cornerstone of a city that was blessed and still is today with the folklore that will soon become apparent within the story that I give to you and all just for the fun of it!

Moving on to the 1950's and on to the time of when 'Teddy boys' and 'Rockers' fought with each other to the sound track of a latter day 'Grease' production. They thrived at this time of indulgence and would form their own gangs around their marked territory which they would fiercely guard at all times with fists of steel. They would try to outdo each other in the name of love by winning the hearts of the many pretty girls around the town with whom they would then fall in love with and then subsequently join in holy matrimony. They would set up home together and then proceed to start a family of their own and all this within the space of one hectic week! The flats were very sought after and offered relative luxury compared to the other 'grots' that were on offer at the time. London Road was awash with public houses with the likes of 'Peppers' or the 'Lord Warden' which were entrenched by people from the locality and where many friendships and marriages were started and even ended on any given night. The Gardens itself was rejuvenated as the last remnants of World War two faded away into the shape of a massive restoration programme. A face-lift of sorts was hastily incorporated that modernised the already modern features and the Gardens were given a new lease of life. A plan was mapped out for the dilapidated but still proudly standing commune that helped change moods and offered vibrancy to the liberated dwellers. They would proceed with many happy times and a future that was heralded for the many hundreds of families who flourished at an unstoppable pace. My mam and dad were growing up in a trove of good times shared with bad times but they prospered when fate finally brought them together in the mid 1960's. It's on to those times now that I will focus my attentions with my brief but informative history of proceedings!

The 1960's carried on over from where the 50's had left off and the beginning of the decade saw the birth of contemporary popular music in the shape of the celebrated 'Merseybeat' era. This saw the birth of bands such as The Beatles, The Searchers, Gerry and the Pacemakers, The Hollies and many other greats who in turn gave a platform to the likes of Cilla Black and the renowned comedians like Ken Dodd and

Arthur Askey. It was a great time to be had by all and fashions changed forever in the shape of miniskirts and a look inspired by the graceful pioneer of fashion herself, Mary Quant. A revolution was taking place and Gerard Gardens was the backdrop of this magical decade and beyond and so would begin my own life story. The 'Mod' movement overtook the Rockers scene and it was a decade that gave way to a massive influx of drugs and free love that carried it through to the 1970's and beyond.

Life was a compendium of 'Beatlemania' and fashion which played a big part in their lives and would always be on show at the 'Cavern' club and the vast array of other haunts like the 'Iron Door' club that would serve the people well in this very fashionable setting. They could now further their own horizons with hope and deliverance and alas 1967, which was the year that the 'Bobster' was to become a new born! This is where my story begins and now heads off into a tandem of spiral delights and many jaunts that were always filled with laughter. These joyous extremities would go on to serve me so well in my own hours of need and detrimental pain. This will be a no directional tale of all of my trials and tribulations that would begin with endeavour and always end up as a crazy adventure. I shall soon reveal more and all in much greater detail as I embark on my ship called 'dignity' in the hope that I might find my mother ship called 'destiny'. I would pursue eleven years of pure nostalgic heaven on my very own doorstep and a stage that was definitely made for me. From that stage I was more than happy to serve the hippy movement of the square with my very own brand of purple haze!

7b, Gerard gardens, Liverpool 3, on the 22nd of April 1967 and in the happy surroundings of a toilet that served me as my makeshift manger. My mother was caught short and 10 minutes later Robert Raymond Parry was born and so my legacy began. From my less than holy crib I would take baby steps forward to stamp my own authority on to a Gerard Gardens that would find a path for me of rich reward and happiness. These great times will never ever be surpassed but I am sure that we can emulate them for our kids in the hope that we can keep such memories alive. Our notoriety will never die or be challenged by anyone who knew this great place and its so many great people who themselves gave so much to our harmonious existence. Growing up in the 'Square' was brilliant for me as it was for my brother and sister who like me and so many others of this golden era will surely testify. We still marvel at our many recollections of what were the happiest days of our lives and we all long for the same things that shaped us up to be what we were at the time and what we have become today. We were the 'New Kids on the Block' who had a story to tell the whole wide world and we would shout it out loud and clear from the slated roof tops that kept us dry. Everyone in earshot would hear what these kids had to say and I am now just putting these words into context that shall remain the true testament of these tenements!

I cannot remember much about my infant years without the exception of me joining my first nursery school along with many of my good friends. The grace and timely intervention of Facebook brought a lot of us back together again and here I am now writing a bloody book to recapture all that has gone before us. We joined forces once more to form our own independent community and it is now thriving with 1000 members and the numbers are steadily rising by the day! My good friend Christine Hanratty created a group called 'old pictures of Gerard Gardens and Crescent' which can be found on Facebook and it really is a must for people to join. We forged ahead at a canter to keep our memories alive and to take them onwards and upwards as the happy community was brought back together again. We are now in touch with each other all the time via the internet and this electronic wizardry has taken us on to another magical level.

Christine invited me to join the group and I was immensely buzzing because the memories that I had kept locked away in Bobby's world were trapped and they really did need to escape. They could now be shared with old friends alike who I thought I had lost forever but who are now my friends again and for that alone I am very happy. I owe a lot to this site and I thank my friend Christine for giving me a platform to tell my own story through my poetry and in my own indelible way. I will utilise and work with the words that I am going to need for this book and I will not struggle to find any words whatsoever because my mind is awash with fabulous cartoon laden memories. I really hope that you enjoy my tale as it is written with love for you all and it is also written with a sincere honesty by me in the hope that my honesty will be my everlasting legacy. I will talk about my first steps as a child and my very first day at school a little later on and I will also mention the many friends who joined me on that fateful first day. That defining day would become my very first day of morning glory and now it's time to tell my story of the forgotten Oasis that once flourished in the pool of life itself!

Bishop Goss formerly St. Josephs and named after Bishop Alexander Goss was my first school and was also the beginning of a childhood that seemed to be basked in a hot sunshine and a vast array of activities. This meant that I was never bored as long as I just basically woke up and threw my kickers on as I made my way down the stairs and into the arena that was our square. It was that easy and we led the simple life that would put today's kids to shame because we really did just get on with it. The school itself was a very imposing building and it is still standing proudly today in almost all of its former glory. Unfortunately the adjoining church has been knocked down since and was a victim of the ethnic cleansing programme that became so apparent in the 1980's. This massive drive was steered to rid the city centre of the tenements and the very people who had lived there for generations! It is a very sore point for me and one that I will not dwell on too much because of its negativity but I must make reference to this wicked act that was bestowed upon us. I want this book to be quite the opposite of doom and gloom and full of great memories that will dominate my account in its entirety.

The iconic St. Joseph's church was built in 1878 (the year that the toffees were born) with the new altar being consecrated in 1881 and the sacred vestments were bequeathed by the parishioners themselves.

They offered various items of gold jewellery including wedding rings and pearls in the wisdom of preserving God in the name of faith and of course to help the holy cause. The church was finally knocked down in the late 1970's due to dry rot that sadly could not be put right and so an institution had perished with devilish neglect being the main factor. The parishioners were unceremoniously herded into a small room which was our former nursery school and it was minute in its comparison to the iconic church that was now reduced to rubble. The 'Station's of the Cross' had been dismembered and now they were being spread out as divinity took a turn for the worse. The desecration of these fabulous buildings was common practice and the word "community" was being systematically crucified by the code breakers of da Vinci! This country is now in an absolute mess because of this massacre of communities and the Holy Spirit has all but vanished from our celebrated faith. I love my faith but I wish that the powers that be would reform their dated way of thinking and bring our church back to its former glory.

St. Joey's was like 10 solid years of summer holidays all rolled in to one and compacted to be preserved into the depths and corridors of my liberated mind. I would just like to interrupt proceedings to say that my beloved mother who passed away on 27th March 2010 is sanctioning every single word that I write and use in this epitaph. My account is written in all of my own words and the accounts given here are what I had personally experienced as a sweet child. My sweetness waivered just a little and I am sure it did with every other child at the time, so sack the raised eyebrows please because all saints have been sinners at some time! I write these fabled words in the hope that my beloved mother will always bless me and keep me safe in times of good and bad and in return I will honour her as any proud son would choose to do. Thanks Pat for guiding me through this book girl and I am sorry for being a little bit of a rogue at times but I have truly mended my ways now and you were always proud of me anyway. I will take that loving notion with me as your final blessing mam and I will continue with what you have taught me to the best of my ability. My story will carry on now with the more engrossing tales of my own nursery crimes and my times of toddler tantrums!

My first day at school was pretty bitter sweet for me because I was leaving behind the golden slumber of 7b Gerard Gardens and now my own bubble of tranquillity had been burst. I soon instilled school life as part of my curriculum and I moved forward at great pace to broaden my horizons. What lay ahead of me was very daunting but it would go on to form my destiny in this dynasty of hidden wealth. It was a massive stepping stone for me and a chance to gain confidence in the presence of others and also the chance for me to succeed in a life that was so full of defining moments. I am actually in the process of just pinching myself with a joy to be finally letting go of the tiger that would eventually become my soul. My beast of burden is now free to wander around the corridors of my mind that were once a very dark place for me but are now illuminated and I can definitely see some light. My happiness was hidden away from me in the tranquil confines of my once redundant memory but now I will use that dormant happiness as a tool to try and get my life back on track for good!

I will now continue where I left off and that was at Bishop Goss and oh what a school of endearment and intrigue it really was. I revelled in this kindergarten establishment for many years along with my participating comrades who themselves joined in the many escapades that were played out on a daily basis. The school can only be described as a 'great' adventure playground that was awash with too many grown ups who were just lying in wait to spoil our alluring times of fun and jest. At worst, they give us rules but my motto has always been that rules are made to be broken! My first memory of nursery school was prompted on that fateful morning when I first met and bonded with my true great friend of those times, Paul Jenkins.

Paul 'Jenko' was a massive influence on me and my life as we shared the whole 11 years together as mates and yes he was definitely my partner in crime. He took my adventures to very different levels that were both innocent to the unsuspecting eye but undoubtedly great in their simplicity and reward! We motored through life and every single day would see us getting up to all kinds of mischief and mayhem. Simple things like climbing the scaffold in our monkey boots or even the odd bit of thieving would make sure that we had sweets galore and remained happy in our very special medium. Paul was hilarious and he would do absolutely anything at all at the drop of a hat and without reason because he was a little bit mad really. It was that compulsion that I loved about him as he would always be the instigator of what we got up to in school and beyond for that matter. I gladly followed suit as I bonded with Paul to join him all the way through my happy tenure of eleven brilliant years spent in the square. It was a friendship that I would go on to cherish for all of my life because Paul gave me so many happy memories and he certainly put lots of devilish excitement into the most mundane of days. Cheers 'Jenko' you are a legend mate and I will carry on now with my journey of endeavours that would behold my very first day at nursery school. My instant memories are of a very tidy little guy, who was pretty shy at first and who would become my very best friend throughout my informative and forever blessed years as a child!

My first day at nursery school will live with me forever as 'Jenko' turned up for class in a smart suit and he really did look the part as I can fondly recall. Other friends who were also starting out on life's endeavours included, Mike Tallon, Paul Hanratty, Gary McHarron, Joey O'Hara, Terry Swann, Paul Woodhouse, Stephen Lindsay, Tony Kennedy, Chris Tremarco, Stephen Tasker, John Melia, Michael Campbell, Kevin Sedgewick and Tommy Grierson. Also on parade from the opposite sex were, Lillian Allen, Maria Muscatelli, Patricia Daley, Margaret Lindsay, Christine Woods and Lesley Smith. Our nursery school teacher was Miss Mctegart and I took my first faltering steps forward as my impending school days would begin in earnest. We all went through the same nursery, infants and junior school together with most of my mates joining me later on at Campion Senior School.

Bishop Goss School was truly immense and steeped in a history of tradition that was both sublime and haunting in equal measures. It was also the very school that all of our own parents had attended and historically theirs before them too. It was always deemed to be a very intimate setting and it is hard to believe that I was more than likely sitting in the same chair that my dad may have used all of those years before me. It was a bit like a conveyor belt for families to follow on in a line of tradition which was 'our' St. Joeys and it was a real honour to keep that line going. Our headmistress was an old biddy called Miss Ford who was a real battleaxe and very strict indeed. She was just like her understudy and her partner in crime at the time who was Miss Keen and together they instilled into us a lot of wisdom. My form teacher in infant school was Miss Rowell and my class teacher was the abundant but sweet Miss Kiely who also acted as the deputy headmistress. Looking back they were all really good teachers at the time and they all made my early years at school a joyous charade. They collectively put me in good stead for whatever may lie ahead in my formative years and I suppose that I have to be grateful of that fact. I am still in touch with Jervais Stringer who was a former teacher in the 1950's and he was present at our reunion night last year. Jervais is thrilled that this book is happening and he will also be present at my book launch!

I always remember the big sand pit in the middle of the classroom which incorporated plastic buckets that had no handles and spades that were also useless because they were so bloody bendy. We would play all morning in that cess-pit before getting our daily handouts of milk and biscuits that were always very welcome and disposed of accordingly. Sometimes they were pretty gritty with the odd grain of sand mixed in to add to the taste but we did not really care. The milk was dispensed in a triangular carton which was delivered in a big orange coloured crate that was in the shape of a ten bob piece but a lot bigger of course. In the summer it smelled a bit like stale cheese which was not very endearing to say the least but we just got on with it because we really did not know any better! The cow juice was freezing cold and it always went down a treat with a Lincoln biscuit or two but we would only get the second biscuit if we were lucky enough and had been well behaved in morning assembly. I also remember making paper mache heads that were made out of balloons and lots of newspaper with dollops of lumpy paste to transform their *News of the World* features. We would create the most hideous faces ever known to man and I felt like of a modern day 'Frankenstein' as I disposed of one that really was coming to life. I am sure that one of them spoke to me so I duly burst the bastard and then hurriedly hid it behind one of the cupboards because I was scared. I reckon that it was one of Mike Tallon's masterpieces because he was always a bit of a rogue himself and this balloon head was just about to explode with fear. Sorry lad!

'May Day' always sticks out prominently in my mind because we would always get done up with pink blossoms and white sheets for 'Our lady'. The Virgin Mary was affectionately termed as the "Queen of the angels and Queen of the May" and we were right up for any celebrations that would come our way. All of the girls in my class (and some of the boys) would clamour around to be the mother of Jesus on this very holy day and I must admit that they truly did look so divine. The girls looked like angels in their full and splendid regalia of lost innocence but that scenario would last for all of one day. The sinners would then transform themselves back into the little witches that they were and the boys would wait for them in their own guises as little devils. Christmas time was also a joyous occasion for us in our infancy because we would always stage a play and every year I would want to be Jesus or Joseph but I would always end up being a donkey. If I was not a donkey then I would double up in some other asshole role that required nothing more than a red face of dejection. I would get on with it though and I would move on to other yuletide activities that were more my cup of mulled wine.

I excelled at making my own unique Christmas tree that would come complete with self made decorations and baubles that would really set my lonesome pine off. They were just twigs that were painted white and they were merrily displayed in a cut down fairy liquid bottle that was then covered in different coloured crepe paper. On completion they looked very seasonal indeed and it was always a joy for me to show off my handy work to my mam in our own little grotto that was 7b. The crepe paper would also be used to decorate the classrooms and I always remember the constant folding of two different colours of endless paper that would transform itself very nicely into a pretty awesome display. My seasonal greetings will continue a little bit later on but first, I have to get through my mountain of schools little creature comforts!

Everybody's favourite pastime had to be cookery but for some reason I can only ever remember making those corn flaky things with chocolate that were so scrumptious and were always eaten in one go! The aroma was blissful and I swear that whenever I walk past Sayers or Greggs I am always tempted in to relive those tasty days of greed. My middle age spread limits me to one every six months now but it is well worth the wait because my indulgences have pretty much become a thing of the past. Easter time would also be a very chocolatey affair for me because we would always make them 'blag' little Easter bonnets. These little treats consisted of a Cadburys crème egg that was laid out on a bed of straw and was surrounded by lots and lots of different coloured mini eggs. For some reason, the cluster of mini eggs diminished rather rapidly as the munchies would set in and our beautifully presented Easter bonnets soon became a straggled bird's nest. Everything in that little bed of straw was eaten alive well before we got out of the school gates and by the time we got home, our little Easter bonnets had turned into broken basket cases!

The school itself was a beautiful building that was teeming with a rich history and a vein of ancestry that went back over 100 years. It was presented with its very own centenary year in 1977 and we really did make a fuss over this fine establishment. This was the same year that was to become the best year of my life by far because apart from our school celebrations, it was also the year that the queen celebrated 25 years on the throne. A massive party was bequeathed on us with all the trappings of a fabulous silver jubilee and we really did know how to throw a proper party back in those days. The jubilee was a massive explosion of red, white and blue bunting that could be seen for literally miles around and it is a story that I will elaborate on in further passages of this book. This also coincided with the hottest summer being recorded in years and at 10 years of age that would more than do me mate! I was very much part of the whole scene at the time and school was not an exception. St. Joey's or Bishop Goss as it was now known was shaping me up very well as a person but academically it was not shaking me up at all. I was not really interested in most subjects at school but I excelled in everything else to do with the English language and of course the literate side of it too.

I remember being in lessons and just clowning around but when it came to English there was no stopping me and I went on to become the best reader and speller in my class. I still have my school report to prove my claims and anyone who doubts my nobleness is more than welcome to a read it. Unfortunately my written work suffered because I had really bad eye sight and it was a dark secret that I duly kept to myself for vanity reasons only. I was like 'Colonel Blink' on glue but I vainly put up with my impairment and just hoped that it would go away but it never did. I did not tell my parents about my problem or my teachers because I feared the dreaded and horribly obscene 'nazzie' health glasses. They were all that were on offer at the time and my vanity screamed out "no thanks" as they were really that bad. I regret that decision a little bit because it really held me back somewhat and reading to the class became a nightmare for me. After attempting to read a paragraph, the words would just 'fuzzy felt' up and I would be left standing there like a right proper tit! All this was happening right in front of my class mates who collectively giggled and made my impaired 'peeps' go even fuzzier. I would suffer the wrath of one 'William Costigan' who was the man who I held responsible for not picking up on the fact that I was frigging blind and he was my headmaster. The signs were there for all to see but obviously I was as blind as a bat and I just suffered in silence as I went on to fail my eleven plus. This would deem me to be a dunce but I was far from being a numskull and I only really excelled when I left school in 1983. On the academic side, the notion of school itself was just a load of old bollocks to me and I could not wait to just leave it all behind me. Having said that, it was also my safe passage in life and an institution that gave me my trusted friends for life!

I loved the other side of school and 'Joey's' was the best school in the world so that was always a welcome plus for me. It was a place where I honed many of my rich talents to make people laugh and I guess that I was pretty much liked by all the kids that stood with me in the playground. I would take my fantasies way and beyond these limited confines and I would gleefully entertain all that was put before me. I never really fought with anyone or had a bad fall out with any of my classmates in my whole 11 years as a 'Gardenite' and my other prolific years as a 'Joey la- la'. If we ever had a scrap then we would keep it for the 'sand hills' at four bells where we would congregate after lessons to settle our many differences. This great school only ever brought me friends and for that reason alone it made my time at this joyous school a massive privilege. Here I was amongst my many good friends as we grew up together in the many summers of love and seldom winters of discontent. I learned to live with the 'Cock eyed nun' and everybody else that I knew at school and they in turn would get to know me very well indeed. I used to love our old caretaker at St Joey's because he was very kind to all of the kids and it was people like him who made our school great. I always remember him making little boats out of balsa wood and he would give them out to all of the kids who in return respected and loved this old handyman. On other occasions, he would let me watch the test cricket in the telly room at dinner time because I was an avid cricket fan and I went on to be an opening batsman for Timbuktu!

Junior school was great and we would hang around in the steaming 'cloakies' when it was pissing down with rain or if it was just freezing cold. We would warm ourselves up by impersonating whoever or whatever was big at the time and I mastered many of my routines in this enclave. The school was pretty strict in those days but I did not care as I just went in, clowned around and then came back home as 'Roger the Dodger' or maybe even 'Billy Whizz'. I always seem to remember the day that I spent as frigging 'Wonder woman' of all people but that confused the shit out of me when I went for a piss standing up! Some of the most hilarious escapades I have ever witnessed took place on my old school steps and they formed part of an act that would bring me so many happy and rewarding times in this celebrated era. It was also the time when I became known as 'Arthur Fonzarelli' (aka) the 'Fonz' and he really was the bees knees. He would lead me into my famed 'teddy boy' era that I both embraced and I elegantly used to shape myself musically as I was sure that I was definitely going to be the next Donny Osmond. I have knocked on many doors for years with my own songs but unfortunately I have never knocked loudly enough because my song writing skills have always been totally abused. My work has been largely ignored by people who are obviously better than me or is it that my songs are just proper shit? Maybe they are just deluded by their own quests for glory and their selfish ways but will they make the grade before me? I guess so because my songs are pretty tame but I reckon if Paul Weller ever got sick, I could easily stand in for him at the Echo Arena. My rock star skills became apparent when I was caught singing 'yellow bird' in those horrible "singing together" lessons that I frigging hated. We all used to sit around a big wooden radio and have to sing to the delights of 'sloop John B' or that knob head of a deep sea diver called 'Quinoro'. I wonder if he ever did find that elusive pearl!

The teachers in my primary care were all characters of their day but my favourite teacher had to be Miss Maher because she was so fit! I spent the majority of her lessons dropping my pencil on the floor and copping an eyeful of her flowery garden that always seemed to be in full bloom. I am damn sure that she knew all about my exploits but she did not seem to mind because after all I was the 'Fonz'. Anything at all was always made possible by this super cool dude and that cool dude of slick presentation was in fact me. Another favourite teacher of mine was Mr Webster who was as mad as a hatter but also a great fellah too. He was driven mad by us and our constant day to day antics of self indulgence and countless hours of total bewilderment. These acts of devilment were systematically dished out to him on a regular basis and I often felt sorry for him as he held his head in his forever trembling hands. The floor in his classroom was a breeding ground for a weird craze that we had developed and there were so many crazes to keep us occupied as the vigour of youth kicked on. Up to this very day I have still not got a clue what it was all about and its origins or even its none apparent earthly meaning. Basically, we would collect all of the broken leads off any coloured pencils that we would scavenge as they nestled in between the cracks of the tar blocked floor. We would endeavour to keep hundreds of these little blighters in our 'toffee laden' trouser pockets but I honestly do not know what we were actually doing it for. We would trade them off to each other with the multi-coloured facets depicting their worth but their true value was basically nothing at all. We termed these little bits of pencil as 'Colditz' and it is at this point of no return where this particular story ends!

Other crazes of the day were those 'big head' thingies that we got from Kitty Carter's and we would stick them on top of our biros or on to our HB lead pencils as some kind of status symbol. They would come in all different fruit and veg guises and if I remember rightly, then the corn one or maybe the banana one was the hardest 'big head' to get. They were easily worth 5 packets of 'Space dust' or maybe even 30 'varnished' Conkers and it really did cost me a packet to develop and nurture my fruity collection. Whoever invented these little plastic characters must be minted now because we must have bought thousands of them in our school alone. The craze swept through the entire city if not the whole wide world and I will bet you that this simple idea led the inventor on to many riches. The biggest craze ever had to be linked to sweets and right up there would be the never disappearing 'Jaw breakers' or the vast different tubes of sweets which included 'Double agents' or multi coloured packets of 'Tabz'. These were little oblong chalky bricks that were made in Czechoslovakia and I do not know how or why I remember that particular fact! 'Doctor deaths' or McGowan's 'egg and milks' would also be on my shopping list as were the not to be forgotten 'Mini bars'. These coconut efforts were little blag 'ruffle bars' that came in different coloured wrappers and displayed a different coloured Mini car on each one. I am in a state of cold turkey now and I am going to have to feed my habit by selling my trusted 'Polyvelt's' to get some 'Spanish gold' from my local confectioner. I can almost taste that coconut tobacco now and I wish that I could get my hands on some of that gear but only for medicinal reasons of course because I am not an addict anymore. To forget my cravings, I am now going back to school and I really hope that this journey will help me to forget all about my past addictions to brown sugar!

Our form teacher was Miss Ratcliffe who was pretty cool really despite the fact that she taught us with a calliper on her leg. It was a fad at the time but the hairy boils on her face were something else and they were retrospectively not so cool. The morning register would be taken and so began another weary day of aimless subjects that were so often blurred by my 'not so apparent' blind panic! The other teachers in junior school were nothing special to me and they were certainly no one to write home about for obvious reasons. Miss Rowell was OK but I just remember her looking like that bird off 'wait 'til your father gets home' with Deirdre (off coronation street) glasses They had not left their lasting mark on me unless of course it was made by the cane and so I considered them to be very boring indeed. We also did a bit of 'Judo' at our school which I was really shite at and I broke my tooth doing a stupid and out of sync rolling break fall. Again it was in front of all my class mates and once again I was perceived as a certified knob as I ambled aimlessly over 'Fizzer' Tremarco's outstretched leg. Mr George just puffed on his pipe and wrote me off as a white belt with three yellow tabs and that is where my colour gradings remained forever. This particular fall from grace would summon the impending demise of my 'Bruce Lee' days and also end the dreams of this particular if not spectacular 'Karate kid'. I considered myself very lucky in having those three yellow tabs though, but if I was to get mugged tomorrow and my skills were called upon for protection, then not even that 'Fonzie' fellah could get me out of that one!

Before I finish my brief encounter with school I would like to make reference to the following people who deserve recognition for the very people that they were and some of whom are forever noted as true legends of their cause. This cause included our nurturing period and ultimately the happiest days of my life and these dynamic people are as follows: Josie D'Annunzio (an absolute all rounder), John Owens (caretaker), Marie Maddox (all rounder), Margaret Taylor (welfare assistant) and of course my beautiful Mother Patricia Parry who would always remain as the complete and utter all rounder plus a million. They worked together with many more great women of their day and helped make this school great with all of the activities that were laid out before us. All of their hard work was so often displayed in a might of abundance that would serve my tribe well throughout our stay at the best school in Liverpool. My book was made possible and has been written with such conviction because of these amazing people who I will thank forever more and of course the countless other great contributors to our more than worthy cause. They were the true warriors of an institution that was chosen for me by God and one that has found its way around my soul to make me very much the person that I am today. It is great just being linked to this amazing chain that carries the weight of solid gold in our unrivalled band of history and truly iconic gems.

The area around our school was also a beacon of enterprise and gave us the 'sand hills' that would be the very place where we would choose to settle our many disputes. We would all climb up mount Calvary until we reached the summit and many a kid was crucified on that plateau I'm telling you! I had a few scraps in my day with the most violent one being with that little tearaway Freddie Woods. We stood for about half an hour just slapping each other across the face until we both got totally pissed off and we decided to have a game of conkers instead. I won and Freddie obliged by buying me a packet of 'football crazy' crisps as we munched our way back to friendship again. The peace would last until maybe the next day and we would act out the same scene over and over again until we got tired and just agreed on not fighting at all. Cazeneau Street was the land that became famously known as 'bubble land' and it got its name from the fact that it was just a mass of molten tar. It would produce water filled bubbles in abundance on a scorching red hot summer's day and it would be a race after school to get to 'bubble land' first. We would burst these bubbles and use the boiling hot tar to make our very own boomerangs that would double up to be very lethal weapons indeed. These self-styled missiles would always come in handy in some way, shape or form and they would often be put into practice by me, expertly or otherwise? They would consist of three lolly ice sticks and three blobs of tar that were great contraptions and just added to my ever increasing weapons of mass destruction. I used these glorified tomahawks time and time again to decimate the 'four squares' on our many days of open warfare. You could launch one of these deadly missiles from the safety of our barracks on the 'ollar' but it would always come back and hit you right on the back of the head with an almighty thud! We would then utilise all our sticky discarded lolly ice sticks to play a game of 'snaps' which involved a little bit of karate and a lot of hard skin on your thumbs. I had a 'Walls ninety-niner' complete with a not so funny joke that was neatly written in little brown letters on the side. It was worth quite a few bob as I recall because it was only one away from being a centurion but somehow, it mysteriously disappeared. Some little bastard robbed it from my desk while I was mooching around in the forever plundered and under siege stock room. I was absolutely fuming and I had my suspects but I could not prove who it was but I reckon it was either Paul Hanratty or Mike Tallon!

This stretch of celebrated land also displayed the old 'Rose Hill' police station which was said to be haunted by 'Mary Kill the cat'. This old witch toured the many maisonettes and the wasteland that stood in our extended vicinity in search of something sinister. This area boasted a whole host of other friends for us who were just waiting to be discovered and like us they really were 'all day' mate! It was said that Mary Herbert lived in this old ruin and at the back of this building was a big hole in the wall that us kids used to climb in and drop down to feed our never ending curiosity. On one occasion there was one of those big red old fashioned meat slicers in the corner and word has it that Mary used this contraption to slice up all the naughty kids and then feed them to her cat. No one dared to ever go in there again but it never stopped me from having a little peek inside every now and then. I would just make sure that no naughty kids were trapped inside this motley chamber of horrors.

The more than mere mortals who aspired from this quaint place were very much like us and they also lived and breathed our easy way of life. We basked in an envious notoriety and in a blaze of glory that would shake my world and theirs as I blossomed wildly with youthful exuberance. From the very seeds of life itself I was steadily growing

21

into one broody sapling and I pollinated all those around me with the sweet scent of laughter. I fed on my own leafy dreams and I matured my way on to the many paths of gold that would lead me from the depths of my conception, to the famous Gerard Gardens itself. These beautifully manicured gardens would go on to be my gardens of Eden and they offered me plenty of fruit that was sometimes of the forbidden kind. I would always bite that rotten apple of sin though, as temptation was religiously delivered to me by the Gods and I was very curious to learn about the teachings of the holy bible.

When Rose Hill police station was made defunct it was replaced by St. Anne Street police station and I always remember my uncle Danny O' Connell working on it as a 'brickie'. He worked for Liverpool Corporation and one day he chased me with his trowel for leaving my signature in the wet mortar that was keeping his well crafted wall together. It was the only statement that I had ever given to the police but unlike Danny's wall it would never stand up in a court of law. The station was opened in a blaze of glory and all of the school kids stupidly went along to an open day that to me was criminally insane. We had our finger prints taken and then we were then put in separate cells for five minutes at a time to maybe curtail our errant ways. I reckon that the 'bizzies' kept most of our finger prints on file to use against us in later years but I was okay because I had put someone else's name on my form and the rest is history so to speak! The 'rozzers' were like the keystone cops but we never saw much of them at all because they were always in the 'Denbigh Castle' getting drunk and disorderly. I would be doing my 'penny for the guy' routine outside of this watering hole and one of them would always say, "Piss off or you are nicked". I heeded their warning to do as I was told by these unlawful men and I would proceed to piss off all over their bloody meat wagon. My truncheon would be put back into place and this particular laughing Bobby would make it home just in time for 'Dixon of Dock Green' or 'Sapphire and Steel'!

We all seemed to thrive in this amazing school of extremities that boasted its very own spooky church and even had its own sacred, if not sacrilegious cemetery. It was a very scary place and also a setting that even had its own resident ghost in the guise of the 'Cock eyed nun' who I swear was always so very real to me. This less than holy figure prompted me to become a huge Christopher Lee fanatic and I was launched into a world of horror that was literally dripping with the blood of this dapper vampire's countless victims. I was an avid subscriber to the 'Hammer House of Horrors' on a Friday night and I fell in love with all of the ghouls and the bloodthirsty vampires that were on the telly at this unearthly hour. They would be seen parading around in some misty filled castle in their most gruesome and ultra grotesque 'guises' of the Count himself and it always seemed more convincing in black and white. You would normally see 'Dracula' or some weird 'mummy fucker dude' running amok with some 'arle' woman's bandages on his head and they would inevitably be chasing some really fit bird. The many victims were chased for hours on end whilst fashioning a big silver crucifix around their necks or a 'blag' spud gun that fired silver bullets. These protective weapons were used in order to kill these grisly ghouls of the night but my favourite implement had to be the stake right through the heart. Many scenes were filmed in the hidden depths of Ealing or Whitechapel of all places and they offered the ghastly scenery that was needed to make you jump out of your skin! It was me ma who introduced me to the likes of Peter Cushing and the gregarious looking Boris Karloff, who in any guise, really scared the shit out of me big time. He was a true master of horror and I loved him to bits as a maniac but I also respected him as a brilliant actor of his time.

I would always look forward to my Friday night trysts with my mother because she would quietly sneak me out of bed and together we would get comfy in front of the rip roaring coal fire. This setting just added to the amateur dramatics that were being expertly played out on the big screen and me and me ma would be in raptures as we pursued the element of fear. With tea and toast for two and the love of my mother all rolled in to one, we feasted on Dracula and Frankenstein as they feasted on the masses of the poor 'down and outs'. These losers would always be looking for a lost mutt somewhere in a weird black and white forest and they all deserved to die because of their stupidity and the fact that they were in Transylvania. This was all carried out behind our Franky and Lorraine's backs as it was also kept from my dad too because it was our little dark secret. The little devil boy that I had become was not telling anyone about our secret manoeuvres in the dark that were cleverly orchestrated by me and my shadow. We had a joint enterprise and it was our own version of 'fright night' that offered me lots of parental guidance in order to keep me safe from these awesome freaks of nature.

My dad worked permanent nights in Otis elevators which was miles away in the outback of 'kiss me quick' Kirkby and we often visited our cousins up there which was pretty cool. It would always be around Christmas time and we always graced them before and after our parties that were held in the massive factory. Ultimately this resulted in me not seeing much of my dad in those days which I genuinely regret but I guess it was just the same for everyone else in the square. At the time he was a really good provider and worked very hard for his now established family and we all so much appreciated his and my mother's overworked benevolence! My mother was a home help amongst other titles and she absolutely loved her work and all the people who she served in a kind abundance. Her kindness towards her patrons was affectionately noted and she possessed a personality that would often leave her revered by everyone who was lucky enough to have met this wonderful woman. I would often go along with her for the ride on my rusty scooter to the many rounds that would take me to meet people like old Mr Clayton. He would always give me an Uncle Joe's mint ball and greet my ma with a mischievous glint in his watery eye. She always looked stunning my mum with her blonde hair and her vast array of miniskirts which at the time, totally 'done my head right in!' All the fellahs in the area would cheekily clock my ma and whistle at her but she would just blush and keep her eyes fixed on me. I would violently erupt as I would throw my dinky car on to the floor and then proceed to offer them all out because it was 'my' mother and she was all mine, okay! One of the worst offenders was Tony Miello who was a bit older than me and he could whistle with no fingers which seemed like magic to me. He did it all the time to just piss me off and I could not whistle back at him unless I had one of them budgie whistles that we used to get in 'Greaty' market. We would buy these little whistles that were made out of leathery wallpaper off some dodgy geezer on his pitch and in an instant we could easily summon a taxi home. My annoyance was somewhat thwarted but I suppose that it was just another compliment to my ma and so now, I am forever grateful to him. My dad was one very lucky fellah indeed and he knew it as he showed her off in the likes of 'Peppers' or the 'Legs of Man' and all of the other pubs that they would visit in and around London Road. She really was beautiful in every sense of the word and I have now been left with a massive void in my life. Without my ma at my side, my life is now so lonely in its entirety but also full of magical memories. It is a void that will only ever be filled with poignant thoughts of the great times that we shared together and the nurturing skills that she taught me so effortlessly. I will carry on my life with her many loving ways running through my veins for all of eternity and I will instil them on to my own two kids, Jay and 'little legs' Eve. They are already on the right road at the moment and thankfully they have inherited her many loving ways. This makes me feel so proud and so very privileged to be known as her son and on the other hand, I am equally privileged for her to be known as my mother!

My school days were littered with mischief and it would always be a double helping of mayhem if 'Jenko' was there. Being with Paul Jenkins was never dull or boring in any way and we really did do some rotten things at the height of our reign. I won't elaborate too much on Paul's little misdemeanours because that would not be fair on him and I am sure that my old mate won't mind my decision in doing this. I have a lot of respect for Paul because he was always loyal to me and without him, this book would have been really dull and uneventful. I thank him for the many good times that we shared together in the hood and I know that our memories will never ever be surpassed as I shall further reveal!

During playtime when my classmates would be out playing 'true dare', I would raid the vacant classroom desks for mainly crisps and sweets. All of the other kids would be busying themselves and doing what normal kids would seem to be doing in a playground but these activities were way beyond my mischievous ways! My booty would consist of rubbers, pencils, rulers, sharpeners, bic biros and basically anything else that had any decent value attributed to it. My main benefactor was a girl who went by the name of Christine Woods because she always seemed to be minted. That was deemed to be not fair by me and it was a case of me robbing the rich to feed the poor. This greedy 'Lone Ranger' masqueraded around the desks like a 'real life' rustler looking for his bounty and for that I apologise profusely. I was not the only rascal about at the time and I could name quite a few but I won't because they already know who they are. I tend to look back at these episodes as just being part and parcel of the 'baby faced' Finlayson act that I aptly displayed and mastered with the greatest of ease. Most of my characteristics came straight out of the *Beano* comic and straight into the cauldron of what was to be, my very own pot of gold!

I was paid back of course, on a number of occasions and one such time was when I brought my 'Scalextric' into school. Some bleeder robbed my two prized cars out of my desk and some of the track went missing too. I was definitely not the only pilferer about at the time because many were the occasions when my own desk would be systematically plundered. It got ransacked all the time and this type of burglary would often leave me totally gutted and totally dejected by my 'would be' aggressor's actions. I hasten to say, that all of you holy innocents reading these tales in horror, need to remember your own very dodgy dealings of exuberance. These dastardly deeds must have served you all pretty well under the circumstances and I bet you all that no confessors will come forward to reveal their own guilty pleasures! It was a case of tit for tat and this tit was definitely going to get his tat back somehow. I would always even up the score no matter who it was and these heists were carried out in pure retribution. Surely 'Jenko' would not stab me in the back and do this dastardly act of betrayal? I was a bit suspicious though when I saw him at Silverstone a couple of years later with Nelson Piquet and James Hunt! I got Paul back by robbing a mouth organ off him from under a cushion in his house but he well and truly got it back. Just as I was getting to grips with this old 'gob iron', it was ripped from my lips by a speeding 'Jenko' and we fell out for 36 and a half seconds. That was the time that it took for us to get back up to his house and delight ourselves with a cup of our specially stewed tea. We would take mischief on to a new level as we replenished our souls with a very cautious approach to authority and another helping of strange brew!

Any spare money that was acquired illegally would be readily spent in Kitty Carter's after school and it would always be jam packed in this little red grotto. 'Bin lids' from all around this vast area would converge on this monument of treats and it was always dead easy to rob poor Kitty blind! This sweet laden paradise smelt just like Sugar Mountain with a mixture of sherbet 'flying saucers' and the delightful 'toffee logs' that used to give me a bad toothache. You could and would buy anything out of this little gold mine but you always had to be careful of her black and white moggy which stank. This pissy pussycat would walk and lie all over the goodies that we were about to receive but I honestly don't think that it put any of us off. The most popular sweets of the day were always displayed on the 'blag' marble counter and thankfully, they would be well within my reach. If Kitty did not stock a particular item which was very rare, then we would trudge on down to Jim Moran's shop by the 'bottom end'.

This area was situated in Gerard Crescent and was adjacent to the flyover on Hunter Street. I only ever went down to the 'bottom end' to knock for Brian Birkett or to swap my 'spam key' with Paul Birchall for a much sought after 'skeleton key'. We would utilise these tools to open up the boots of the cars parked by Transport House and we would rob the spare wheel to push it down Hunter Street. If we were lucky then we would cop for a bag of spanners that we would use for ermmmmm! Nothing whatsoever! Jim Moran's was around the corner from the youth club that offered us the delights of boxing and sweet disco infernos. It also gave us the many other various activities that would keep us out of trouble and we would be really decent kids albeit for an hour. This club would go on to feed my lust for life and it was at its height in those forever hazy, shady, lazy, days of summer. We played to the rhythm of 'Queen' and rocked to the beat of the 'Bay City Rollers' as a tartan invasion threatened the status of my idols, Showaddywaddy! I did not really knock around the 'bottom end' but I had other mates there including Damian Kelly, Eddie Lester and Charlie Moore who sadly passed away last year. I enjoyed some fun times with Charlie Moore and he was a big player in my 'copper wire' exploits. Charlie was always game for a laugh and we made quite a few quid out of the copper wire but his biggest sin was to borrow candles from Holy Cross Church so we could sit off in a 'bombdie'. Great day's lad and they will be forever etched in this book of sinful deliverance. Rest in peace mate and I promise you that I will light a candle for you, but I might just borrow it from my local church for the sentimental irony of it. Ha Ha!

I also seem to recall an incident when our Lorraine and her mates including Ann-Marie Welch, Stella Melia and Catherine Fay robbed a box of KP crisps from the once again under siege stockroom. They stuffed the bags down their knickers to hide them and then they continued on their merry way until they were confronted by me. I asked our Lorraine for a packet of smoky bacon and in return I would not squeal to the authorities but she foolishly refused point blank! The very next day I blew her up to 'Pontius' Costigan and she also got the dreaded cane for her troubles but she would soon forgive me. My errant ways of blackmail and treachery were very rewarding but I never grassed on anyone ever again because grassing was bad and I had committed a very big sin. It was simple really and she should never have crossed me in that way because it was evident that I was an all round baddie but I did not mean to be. I grew out of my baddie patch and most of the time I was an angel who was always eager to please everyone who I loved. People seemed to like me around our parts because I did my own thing and I was notably full of charm in order to get my own way. More importantly for me it was a confined logic to get my own payday which was sometimes paramount to everything else that mattered. I was a 'lone ranger' at times but whenever I needed my 'silver' then my trusted horse would always be by my side. We rode around this town looking for our 'gold rush' and he would always be ready, willing and so very able, as he waited diligently for my next solitary command. After a few more innocent but illegal gigs me and Paul just went back to our safe hunting grounds but we never really over stepped the mark and being little villains was by far the worst thing that we had ever done. I will always look back on these 'petty theft' times with a sense of benevolence and a sense of utter joy!

Crime was never a big issue in these melancholy days and I think that the only time I ever saw a police car was when Eddie Yeats got chased through the arches by an RS 2000! They must have been filming a scene for Coronation Street or maybe it was just another figment of my often vivid imagination. I really do not regret any of my actions for one moment or any of the many escapades that I embarked upon in what was to become a decade of pure decadence. The only exception I would hang my head in shame over was maybe grassing on our Lorraine but she would always get me back somehow or some way!

Me and 'Jenko' were both into bands called 'Showadywaddy' and 'The Darts' who we both loved at the time and it was Paul who taught me the famous 'ted dance'. He was a great dancer and soon his toe, heel, toe moves would be instilled in me forever as we stormed the dance floors on our quest to be the best. We would both go to St. Joey's disco where we would perform our choreography to the likes of 'Hey rock and roll' or 'Under the moon of love' as we were immersed in our 'Teddy boy' heaven. I ended up buying a pair of crepe sole shoes to add to the look and on one occasion I was tempted to apply a full tub of Vaseline on to my vast flowing locks. My transformation into a 'teddy boy' was now complete and this rock god was ready to roll. My ma went ballistic because it was the type of Vaseline that was dispensed for chapped lips and not the one that my dad would use on his ever tidy but greasy bonce. It was nothing like that blag 'Brylcreme' that my Dad used in the shocking days of winkle pickers. My dad was always dressed smartly and he sported his very own wispy quiff which was always immaculate. He also incorporated a Donald Duck arse to match and I must admit that he looked very cool in every sense of the word. It was a look that I tried to emulate with but unfortunately my appearance was that of a 'lard arse' and I only ever repeated this charade again with water or sweat. I was in dreamland and I just rocked the night away like some crazed 'Tasmanian devil' on speed balls. It took me many weeks and lots of carbolic soap to finally get this tubby mess out of my hair and eventually my head was returned to its former glory as a bowl and that was that! My 'bowl head' look was inspired by 'Cotter' the 'barbarian' and he was responsible for many bad hair days. He really was a head wrecker in every sense of the word and I was absolutely terrified of him.

'Cotter the barbarian' was supposed to be a barber but he was definitely a butcher and he should have been one of Hitler's henchmen. If I was naughty then I would have to go to Cotters with my dad where my punishment would always involve this hair criminal giving me the dreaded 'bowl head' look. I would sit there sweating profusely as I waited for my turn and I observed the many victims that would reluctantly go before me. It was a cruel process but it was done with such dignity in the face of adversity and I will never forget the look of terror in the many victims haunted eyes. That same dignity was quickly turned into abject horror when the results of this mad man's carnage were revealed in the big mirrors on his wall. The many casualties of this atrocity still bear the deep scars today as a constant reminder of this man's quest for supremacy. I think that the aggressor in question is now living in safe exile that is both a tax haven for this dictator and also a place for him to claim 'fringe' benefits. He is a wanted man for the indiscriminate acts that he performed on the many 'bowl heads' that wandered around these poppy fields aimlessly. As a result of his despicable hair crimes many of my friends including me have now opted for the baldy look. A monument has since been erected in Soho Street to commemorate the many fallen victims of this one man crusade who were cut down and subjected to this man's heinous 'black adder' dressage. These vile atrocities were carried out in the name of the despised 'German helmet brigade' who were unceremoniously cut down by the fearsome 'Crew cutters'. The altercation was fought out on the big 'ollar' and the 'Crew cutters' prevailed in this famous battle of the mullets. 'Cotter' still remains at large and there is now a bounty on his head as he faces the prospect of a 'hair crimes trial' in The Swiss Supreme Court.

My 'electric legs' dance moves were legendary but it was 'Jenko' who was the master of our craft and he craved all of the attention. I can enviously remember that there would always be a big circle of girls around him but I was waiting patiently in the wings and my time would eventually come around. He was always really nifty on his feet which in turn served us both well with the girls and at the age of seven or eight I was more than ready. There would be plenty of girls who would fall for my undying charms at a glance but I was always very choosy. I will leave that one well alone for now because I am in fear of any reprisals that I might encounter from all of the hearts that I may have broken in my heyday! St. Joey's disco was legendary and definitely the highlight of our week that was jam packed with things to do at our leisure. My life was just an explosion of fun times and the organised chaos that often ensued was just an added bonus! My walk out of childhood and into the heady heights of being a grown-up had begun and here I was, ready to take on the whole world. I walked the square like a mini 'James Cagney' or that well hung lothario who was better known as Erroll Flynn. This dirty rat of a hoodlum was already looking around the town for a sweetheart to call my own and to finally tame my wild ways. I would trawl the seedy joints around the Lime Street area including the notorious 'Aladdin's Palace' or maybe that 'Las Vegas' joint that was under prohibition at the time. Even that 'Monte-Carlo' gaff was off the beaten track but that was fine by me because it was a right den of iniquity. This joint offered me a permanent base and a crew of trusted lieutenants who turned this hoodlum into public enemy number one. I was not fazed though because my public enemies were only the tramps and the beggars of my world which was pure fantasy at its best. The real world was always too boring for me and I continued to act out my fantasies on the biggest stage of them all. The lure of the bright lights was too much for some kids but this 'good fellah' could handle the situation with ease. It was always teeming with broads who were eager to put out and the talent on show was always exceptional as I fondly recall. I was my own boss and I answered to no one except for that dude up in the sky because he scared me. The 'big man' had given me my faith and the beliefs that I would always harbour in my criminally insane mind. I was still only 8 or 9 years old at the time but I already felt way beyond my years because it really was all happening for me. I just loved the fact of who I was and what my life in general was becoming because my escapades provoked my youth which was absolutely brilliant!

Junior school continued to be eventful and I look back on these days in awe as to how good the memories actually were. They sometimes still overwhelm me as they take over my mind like a rancid rash of undiluted nostalgia. These inhibitions could only be felt by a child who came from this sacred place and I was happily living out my dreams in the full glare of my respected peers. Every day was just another episode for me and I thrived on all things fun as I acted them all out to perfection. The boring kind just nodded their disapproval with a nudge or a wink but that just spurred me on to go one step further and I probably always did. It was a magic roundabout of happiness that is present in every single step and breath that I take today, but in an otherwise mundane and ordinary existence. I suppose that I am wasted now and maybe I should have been an actor instead of a writer or maybe even both. I would give anything to be an actor because everything would be so very natural to me and be a complete and utter breeze. My chance will come but in the meantime, I will just plod on with my dreams and hope that one day I get my opportunity. I had a bit part role in a new film that is coming out in December and it follows the trials and tribulations of both Everton and Liverpool FC respectively. It was a hoot to do and it really is going to be a cracking film because I am in it and I know how funny it is going to be. It was produced by Dave Kirby and it is the follow up to the critically acclaimed "fifteen minutes that shook the world" which charts Liverpool's more than lucky exploits in the European cup final. The new film is called "Reds and Blues: The Ballard of Dixie and Kenny" and my part was filmed in a fictional pub called "The Bitter and Twisted Arms". I had an absolute ball doing this film and I reckon that I will get even more than my allotted five minutes of fame. Look out for my 'extra' role at Christmas when the DVD will be available for retail in Red and Blue covers that were cleverly implemented to keep the warring factions apart. I did not get paid for any of the contributions that I made to this film and I am plugging it to get an invite off Dave Kirby to the film premiere at Liverpool one. If you are reading this book Dave then do the decent thing mate because I think that you know the script and you probably got this book for nothing anyway. Ha Ha! Good luck with the film lad and maybe I will get spotted in my loutish role by Quentin Tarantino but knowing my luck it will probably be that Quentin Crisp fellah. I am going back to my original script now because I am completely losing myself in this web of intrigue and I have got many more stories to be getting on with!

We were only fledglings at this great time of the 1970s but we knew the score and junior school gave way to the many influences that would shape me up into the form of my most influential idols. Superstars like the iconic and ultra cool 'Arthur-Fonzarelli' were very influential figures to me and being him was definitely a step forward into my many 'happy days'. This life changing show was on at around tea time after the Bay City rollers gig so you could not really ask for more in these fine days of oblivion. I always did though because I was always a bit of an Oliver and I wanted more, more and more again! Everybody wanted to be the 'Fonz' and that included me because he was so cool and so bloody good looking. I tried my best to mimic him but it went the same way as my other alter ego 'Steve Austin' AKA 'the bionic man' or the critically acclaimed 'six million dollar man'. I was convinced that I was Steve Austin and both my mam and dad used this fact to totally pull the wool over my less than bionic eyes. They would ask me to go on all kinds of messages in wind, rain, hail and snow and they would time me on a 'blag' Mickey Mouse watch that did not even work. I could not even tell the time because I only had my 'Casio' digital watch so they really did have me off big time. I was always convinced that I was getting faster by the day and never in a million years did I ever think that in fact it was just another big fat lie! Off I went on my bionic rounds of industry and benevolence in search of my many deluded powers but my powers were being controlled by the deceitful powers that be. It seemed so real to me because I was lost in a world of pure fantasy and it was only ever my mam and dad who managed to completely hoodwink me. I would often be seen sporting my personalised Bionic man tee shirt and I would be gone for what seemed to be ages but in reality it was no more than maybe four minutes or so! On my flustered and out of breath return they would be counting 18...19...20 and I would be eager to beat my record of 25 seconds. They would take a second off my personal best each time I ran an errand, just to make me believe that I was truly bionic and this not so clever dude fell for it hook, line and sinker. Absolute class folks but I would also pull the wool over their eyes on so many occasions in my quest to be a real superhero!

I got the gist of their untruths after about 3 years and I kicked my bionic leg in to touch as I moved on to being 'Bodie' or 'Doyle' out of the professionals! Anyway, I was already the 'Fonz' so it did not really matter that I was no longer bionic because I was so cool and trendy and a bit of a stud for the vast array of chicks in my midst. My name was scrawled all over the school desks and emblazoned on all of the walls around the square. They were happy to incorporate such notoriety and self prominence and not one wall ever escaped my felt tipped pen. I really did try to emulate this dude because all of the pretty girls on my list loved him for his looks and of course his utter coolness. Instead of having a leather coat and the cool 'Brutus' jeans that my authentic look and outfit required, I opted for the less appealing and even less convincing 'snorkel' and pair of black velvet

34

'kecks'. The velvet monstrosities were part of my communion suit and they haunted me for years until I found a way to destroy them forever. My look did not really match that of Henry Winkler's but I did not care because I was in my own world and I was acting out all of my heroes and villains in their various and often 'iffy' disguises. St. Joey's and Gerard Gardens gave me the perfect stage to be whoever I wanted to be and I wanted to be everyone at some point or other. One day I was 'champion the wonder horse' or 'Stan Laurel' and the very next day I would be in my element as 'Tom Sawyer 'or even one of the 'Banana Splitz' if I so wished!

The Gardens were absolutely blooming in the 1970s and it was definitely my time and the crowning glory of all what was going on around me. I was living in this 'flower power' and 'rose tinted' spectacle of any era gone by and I was thoroughly enjoying my time as a resident gardener. My family was cool and I would see all of my aunties and uncles and my many cousins all of the time. We were always very close knit and we often lived in each other's pockets because every door was considered to be an open door. I especially enjoyed Saturday nights because my mum and dad would go out to one or more of the local haunts that were dotted around the London Road area. At closing time, the whole Parry clan would descend upon us as it was all back to 7b for a party. We would get up and sit in the smoke logged kitchen as it was then known and we also had a back kitchen which is unheard of in these days of relative luxury. Anyway it was the perfect setting for an almighty parry shindig and there would be many good times as the heady days of the 70s flamboyantly rolled on. This more than merry clan would all take it in turn to belt out a classic tune and sometimes the songs got well and truly murdered. More often than not, we were treated to a really good rendition of 'For the good times' by Perry Como or my mum's sweet version of 'Rose garden'. My favourite song by my mother was 'Sing me an old fashioned song' by 'Skeeter Davis and I often performed this song in the back of a black hackney cab. It even gets the taxi drivers singing and they always end up giving me a handsome tip. I won't tell you what that tip was but it always ended with the more than subtle words of "Now eff off"! This was a defining time for me in becoming a massive 'Como' fan for life because every time I hear his voice it just takes me back to these magical moments and to a time when my heart was free from any pain whatsoever! I felt honoured with all that was bestowed upon us by people who were lucky enough to be living in such splendour at this very exciting period of time. We marvelled at these intimate gatherings that were spent in affordable grandeur so to speak and I have lots of great memories of the many antics that were to present themselves before me. We did not have much but what we did have was ours and we respected that fact because above all, we were all very happy just to have our families!

It was a time that was really tough for people from all walks of life but everyone just mucked in together to make it the place that I fondly recall. I will never ever let this great place be forgotten and I hope that my journey will somehow reawaken this sleeping giant. We witnessed a well being and a sense of security that was not found anywhere else in the city with the honoured exception of the many other great tenements in our area. They were mainly scattered around the city centre at the time but could also be found in the various parts of this great dock land called Liverpool. Holy Cross was another great parish that prospered alongside us and served our community so well. I hung around the tenements of Vauxhall Gardens, Fontenoy Gardens and Portland Gardens respectively which were also very close to my heart because I made quite a few friends in these hospitable confines. These great tenements housed our many neighbours and friends that were littered about the world famous 'Scottie Road.' This vast area was very much a part of us as we were also very much part of them and this was so often displayed over our many years of togetherness. The area around Comus Street will also get mentioned because they too were very much part of us and I was so proud to be amongst all of these great communities. We lived together side by side and existed in such harmony that it was hard to believe really. Being the greatest community in the world was so heart-rending because there was only one Gerard Gardens and we were proved to be the best crew on the whole planet bar none. It belonged to us and we made the most out of these great gardens because to do otherwise would have been a complete travesty. I did the lot to excess in most cases because I was always hungry just to learn and earn my way out of my childhood. Stepping into adolescence was very easy for me and I carried my crusade forward at an unstoppable pace. The mellowing times rolled smoothly on and the partying had only just begun at 7b Gerard Gardens!

The Saturday night parties went on forever all over the squares but it was the perfect backdrop for me to get a few bob off my more than generous aunties and uncles. The many spirits would fill the room and the gang of them would be conclusively drunk but they would always be great company in their own individual ways. They would ask us kids to give them a song while they were being embalmed with scotch whiskey or whatever else that would be on offer at the time. We would accept their requests and make a show of ourselves for five minutes but that five minutes would often turn into five pounds worth of slummy. They were all very generous to us and they will always have our respect for that fact amongst the other like-abilities that would often shine through. My mother would look after everyone and kept the liquor flowing from the makeshift bar on display. The bar was hastily set up in the back kitchen and you could not swing a cat in there but we always managed to throw a good party no matter what. It was brilliant seeing all of my family together singing and laughing in unison while including us kids in an almighty blast. On the odd occasion there would sometimes be a minor scuffle which would normally end up with my dad getting my uncle Robbie or Jimmy in a headlock. A fisty-cuff would normally ensue over someone maybe crucifying a rendition of one of the many classic 'croon tunes' that were very much a part of these social gatherings. These original X factor shows were taken very seriously indeed and inevitably someone would get the bullet for singing hideously out of tune. The effs and blinds would continue down the stairwell and in to the square but it would be done and dusted in a matter of seconds. All would be forgiven and then forgotten until they would meet up again the next week and so the happy cycle of events would continue to roll on, in near perfect harmony. Life just moved on for us and was beset by the never ending summers and picturesque winters that just added colours and unique events to behold any cherished memory!

I would hold on to and fondly lock up all of these memories for a very long time and put them safely away into the cockles of my heart. They nestled at the very back of my mind and now they are being unleashed via this book that is teeming with great memories. It is only lately that I have started to release these great memories in the form of poetry and poems are another book I'm afraid but it will happen sometime in the near future! My new found friend is nostalgia and my mantle is now being exclaimed within the realms of this book. I sincerely hope that my words are coming across to you all in the right way and I pray to god that this journey will open the doors of happiness to me. I will grasp this gem of a chance with open arms to prevail my worth as a writer which in turn will reveal itself in this oath of my many happy chapters. I am really pleased with my effort up to yet so please just enjoy my work at your own leisurely pace!

I continued to prosper along the passage of life with a sense of purpose and endeavour to build my own dreams in this fascinating amphitheatre that was laid out before me. The magnificent setting and grace of Gerard Gardens was awe inspiring and continued to feed my rapid development.

The summer holidays were always very special to me and completely epitomised the greatness of my lucky and cherished childhood. Every day was an adventure to be had and boy did we manage to exhaust every single minute of every single day that was on offer to us. My time was littered with days out to Morecambe or Blackpool on the legendary 'Charabancs' which where the luxury coaches of their day. They were a form of transport that served us well on our many days out with our own chief organiser of fun being the one and only Angie Volante! It seemed like the whole square was on the bus and it was a chance for us to escape the four walls of Gerard Gardens and clock the sights that would normally only be accessible to us via the odd postcard. We were out for the day and we would unleash our wit and charm on to the 'woolybacks' of the great or not so great northern hemisphere better known as Manchester! Blackpool was always awash with these scruffy 'stud in the nose beauts' and we always had them off for their 'Sally Webster' birds. I think the birds loved us because we were dead trendy and none of us ever sported one of those porno style muzzie's! We would not be crossed by anyone at all and we solemnly protected our status as we toured the coastline on our many famous days of liberating sunny travels!

Our days out were often an open adventure and it was a chance for us to show off our new found independence. We would put into practice our experience as we crafted many free gifts from all of the little shady shops that we would seek out and pilfer along the way. The journey would always culminate in the singing of a very hearty song or two with the old time classic 'in my Liverpool Lou' setting the pace. These intimate songs stood the test of time to become a regular, but sometimes prolonged ditty, that would get us all singing along. We would all join in to get into the mood that would set us up for our long day ahead and I truly loved these days out with all of my best mates.

Our brief encounters with the coast would always be great with all of the penny arcades on show and the many sand dunes that would serve me well as a bit of a heartbreaker. I always remember my mam waving us off and giving me a couple of bob to go on the fair and maybe have a crack at the donkey derby which was definitely a fix. I would religiously bring her a present back home that I had probably nicked off the gypo's on my many rounds of 'waltzer' glory. We masqueraded through the house of fun with a madness that was mirrored everywhere we went and our crazy capers often got us into trouble. My days of mischief were often fuelled by candy floss and the iced doughnuts that my hypo sugary appetite would require. I got out of any jam that I would often find myself in with the girls by just sweet talking these silly tarts around and I would always end up getting a nice slice of their cream pie. I never went for jammie dodgers because they were so bloody gooey and I always opted for something a little more tempting like their cherry bakewells. I always returned the favour by giving them a piece of my cheesecake and we all lived happily ever after!

Even if me ma was skint, and sometimes she was, she would always make sure that we had the same money and clothes as all the other kids and this was a pattern with my mam that would repeat itself time and time again. We were never ever sacrificed for any of the ends or means that were so prevalent in our day and may have occurred to her from one day to the next. She was always eager to see to it that we did not ever go without the basics that we needed to survive in these futile times of genuine hardship. I never quite suffered the ravages of poverty because I was spoilt rotten as a child and if I have to be perfectly honest, then we led a somewhat sustained lifestyle that our parents had made us accustomed to. They even went on to sport their own matching fur coats at the weekend which I am sure were the result of Snowy Robbo's many illegitimate pups. That is another story for me to tell in this book of puppy dog tails and I will reveal all about 'Huggy Bear' a little bit later on. It's back to Blackpool now for more helter skelter fun and the scream that we had on our ghost train of endeavours!

We would literally take Blackpool by storm as we waded in to the fun fair and the glare of what was the amusement arcades. They were a treat to the eye and it really was another world to us and one that we made the most of on our epic and endless days out at the seaside. After a day of thrills and spills we would make the safe journey back home to Liverpool 3 where my ma would be waiting for us with a portion of chips from Gianelli's and a smile bigger and wider than the Mersey tunnel itself! There were no holidays abroad at this time and a week in Torquay or Blackpool was as good as it got for most people but I was a very lucky exception who was about to embark on a voyage of discovery. I got my passport to freedom via my uncle Robbie and my aunty Marie Heston who both doted on me when I was just a nipper. We took in countries such as Spain, France, Portugal and even some of the more exotic places of the world like parts of Africa. It was in these far off shores where I earned and was stuck with the nickname of the self hating acrimony termed as monkey's bum! The name came about as I got badly sunburned on my milk bottle chest and the scorch marks resembled some kind of baboons arse. I don't know who landed me with this nickname but I guess that it may have been our kid!

My uncle Robbie was a Member of Parliament for our area and he served the community well but served me even better as a kid. I packed my 'cozzie' and towel for my mega jaunt in preparation of self discovery as I was soon to find out and in the best possible way imaginable. They could not have any kids of their own so they sort of adopted me for five weeks as I accompanied them on this once in a lifetime jaunt that would live on with me forever.

We travelled by car and boat but it was brilliant just taking in all the different ports and sampling the vast array of continental food and drink that were on offer. It was a mammoth experience and one that other kids could only ever dream about but it was really happening to me. I remember one night in France when I staggered from table to table after polishing off the remnants of some fine bubbly that I had found at my drunken leisure. I ended up as pissed as a fart and I was trying to flirt with all the gorgeous French chicks in sight of my blurred vision. It all came to no avail of course and I was left nursing the effects of the 'whirlie's' for the first time ever. We boarded the night ferry to 'viva Espana' and the choppy sea did nothing at all to help my underage drinking spree that left me in a right state. I spent the whole journey being seasick but it was well worth it and I was fine by the time we had disembarked. Here I was at just 5 years of age and already I was on the rampage and seemingly beyond my infantile years. I swash buckled around the dimly lit decks of this massive boat and turned into 'Long John Silver' to alleviate any boring moments. I was actually featured in the catholic pictorial as I left a trail of candles at Lourdes and I was the envy of all my mates on my return back home to the cradle. I also went on many jaunts with Robbie to the House of Commons where I would often leave a gift for Margaret Thatcher. I would present my parcel to this 'milk robber' in the communal area which was in fact the shit house and I made sure that it was carefully wrapped up in bog paper. I could not think of a more appropriate location to leave this iron lady a parcel that was sometime's hand delivered. My return to dry land coincided with a head full of red lice and a monkey's arse that was tattooed to my chest and would live with me forever. They were to be my only souvenirs of this incredible and life changing 'bon voyage' and I was glad to eventually get rid of them!

I headed back to the relative doom and gloom of the square that lasted for no longer than a day until I got back in to the swing of things. I quickly realised just how much that I had missed and really loved this endearing place and it did not take me long to find my feet again. It was great just to be back amongst my friends and the trappings of a place that I was truly and madly in love with. Other days out with my mam included New Brighton and Crosby where we would spend all day picking cockle's on the beach. Me ma would peel off to relax with her flask of tea as she topped up her long awaited sun tan. A bronzy would make her look even more beautiful than she already was and with our little black leather radio turned on we would tune in with ourselves and with the air waves that were all around us. They would gleefully beckon me on at every abated breath of fresh sea air that I took in and I was lost in a seaside of euphoria. I would just want to run wild and take everything in that was on offer to me and was refreshingly free from the pollution of a city centre tenement block. New Brighton was also a big adventure to us because we would get to go on the big ferry and across the famous River Mersey. We would then walk on to the indoor fair which was mega and then on to the very imposing and invigorating outdoor baths. The open air pool always offered us kids a splashing time in all kinds of adverse weather that would seem to accompany us everywhere we went. It would either be pissing down with rain or baking hot in glorious sunshine but that fact did not bother me because we would just make the most out of being out at the seaside on our mini summer holidays!

We hastily lapped it up in the more warming and energy sapping hot sunshine that was seemingly apparent on these great days out. I guess that I took the sunshine for granted despite the odd day of rain that would see us confined to the indoor fair! We were really spoilt for choice and as ever my mother would make it all the more special with her carefully prepared marmalade butties. She would make them in the morning and by dinner time they would be readily handed out accordingly. They would always go down a treat with a melted 'breakaway' and a gargle of flat Iron brew that would give us all of the energy that we needed on these fruitful jaunts. I always remember the 'lanny' (landing stage) being absolutely chocker with ravenous kids and mums alike as we all were rabidly eager to get on to the bustling and forever swaying ferry. *The Royal Iris* just wheezed and bristled with the sheer number of hungry seasider's that graced its open decks in the splendid sunshine. I was often very surprised that the landing stage did not sink as the masses of people turned it in to a not so floating piece of wood. When we returned home from our days out in the sun we would be absolutely knackered and we would lash all of our cockles into a massive pan of boiling water. The screams would be unmerciful and sometimes it sounded like girls running away from me in a game of 'kiss and tell'. The poor cockles would be drowned in a mass of malt vinegar just to make sure that these little crustaceans were in fact dead and then we would gobble them all up for a very authentic fishy supper. My love affair with vinegar was compounded and I used this trait to put loads of this 'blag' wine on to anything that resembled fish and chips. My old mate Austin Muscatelli and his gorgeous wife 'Josie' termed me with the nickname of "Vinegar Joe" and this little label stuck with me for many years. These two brilliant people were definitely the 'salt and vinegar' of the earth and together they both served me well as Johnnie Gianelli had served me a couple of years before. The long days encapsulated everything that was good about my life then and they are the days that I so often long for now. I try to relive these magical days with my own 2 gorgeous kids but for some reason it does not quite seem to be the same. The times have changed unfortunately and all at an alarming rate it would seem. Gone forever are the lost days of innocence that have now sadly been replaced by a world that is so full of worry and concern over what lies ahead for our own kids. I suppose that this is just the fact that I am now a parent in a world that seems so far removed from the one that I remember as a child!

I am a third of the way through this epic tale now and I hasten to pause but I need a little time to reflect and take stock of what I am going to write next. I have worked for six solid days and nights now and I am feeling a little weary as I exhaust my mind for all the hidden treasure that I will inevitably unleash. I don't know which direction that this fabled account of my life is going to take next but I solemnly promise you that it will become even more engrossing for you to read. It is time for you to get lost again as you breeze through the remaining pages of this eye-opening book. My wish is to now tempt you in to my world as I take your hand and lead you down memory lane one more time. We can reminisce together as we head off back to the days of a relentless happiness in the relative safety of an armchair. This book will really open up your mind and my story will now take shape to be moulded as a 1970s relic. I assure you that it gets even better as my adventures continue at such pace and purpose in this labyrinth of love and I will give you more fascinating tales of my pleasure seeking exploits. Grab yourself a box of 'after eight' mints and demolish them completely with a cold glass of R White's lemonade as my tales now continue in earnest!

I can safely say that every day spent in Gerard Gardens was different and offered me a multitude of activities because this colonial compound was always blessed with things to do. Even if it was just a game of British bulldog or a cry of "put your hands in the bucket if you want to play cowboys and indiaaaaaaaaaaaaaans", we would never run short with our aspirations for fun. The more subtle games like 'toilet bingo' were a joy to behold as we would wait for a row of toilet lights to go on in descending order as we sat by a fire in the middle of square. These fires were routinely made up of newspaper and an endless stream of wood and milk crates that we robbed from the Miller's mobile van or the easier target of Barney's. This little sweet shop was another institution and another 'sweat shop' that my ma worked in for many a moon. It was also very handy for the many obvious reasons but I had my poor ma harassed for packets of 'tiger tots' and anything that would appease my insatiable quest for chocolate. We would play 'toilet bingo' for literally hours on end because it required a lot of patience and a really keen eye to see over the toiletry proceedings. When we got our line of toilets or the four corners that were required to win, we would all sing out in unison "Mary Mary, get off the bog,--------- Mary!--------- Get off the bog!" Now I only use the name Mary as an example and I am not being personal to anyone called Mary because it's just a good old fashioned name and it also happens to be the name of my gorgeous nana Shields. I am sure that 'Nellie' would not mind my minor indiscretion because you are all in really good company. My nana was a brilliant woman who totally inspired me and others around her with her sharp wit and her very sharp tongue. She would leave everyone in hysterics with her put downs and definitely could grace any stage that was put before her.

We would sit-off for hours by the fires with all the older lads that included Sosky Roan, Strodie, Barney O 'Rourke, Tony Miello, Biffo and many more who I could name but can't really be arsed doing so. There are way too many of you to list so geg out and stop trying to steal my thunder because this book is about me ok! It would be us 'youngie's' who would keep the fires going and we would sit there for ages just amusing ourselves by throwing the odd aerosol on to the fast failing fire. This explosion of hair lacquer fumes would scatter the ashes everywhere and would help to generate a bit of a whoosh for the now dying embers. Our pyrotechnic display enabled the molten ashes to readily reignite themselves again and we would have to keep the fire going with a steady supply of plastic milk crates. This routine would repeat itself most nights and we kept the wintry elements at bay by fashioning these outdoor fireplaces. All of the mothers would be seen on the landing doing what mothers do by having a good old jangle with the neighbours. They would gab until it was time for us to go in and I would settle down with my customary delight of tea and toast which was done on one side by the coal fire. Before bed time I would reflect on my endeavours and my eventful day would draw to an end. "Goodnight mum", would be my last words as I would toddle off into my bedroom for a much needed sleep and a chance to recharge my exhausted batteries!

We played out in the square until all hours because it was safe and the vast playground that was our square was illuminated with the installation of our very own 'Match of the day' football stadium floodlights. This electric shock of light would in turn give us a 24 hour football pitch and a fascinating playground that was host to all manner of scrapes and great adventures alike. I loved playing football and we would have matches against the Crescent all the time that would sometimes be completely over the top. We played with the old orange 'Master 5' balls that I would often volley over the bar with my trusted right foot. I would find help with the grace of my Dunlop 'Red flash' trainers which were the Adidas 'Predator' of their day. These 'flash in the pan' efforts were a hand me down off our Lesley and I sported them with immense pride because they were so trendy. Lesley was my cousin and she lived in 'Cannibal Farm' that was to be the happy setting for my many summer holiday visits. She was very instrumental in my trendsetting days because of her love of bubble coats that replaced those horrible budgie jackets. Her and our Lorraine were more like best mates but they would always try to outdo each other with their bad kilts and pairs of 'Cornish pasties' that would be bought from 'greaty' or Ravel in the precinct!

I was pretty crap at football and had to reluctantly give way to the likes of Gary McHarron or Brian Taylor who were pretty decent at the beautiful game. They would always give me the run around which would often leave me in the shade and in a bamboozled state of affairs. Kevin Keegan even lived in our square but I can never remember this special 'K' ever performing a nutmeg on me because I was too quick for him. David Brady may have suffered this indignity because he was the pick of the bunch and football was never quite his game. We loved playing football against the Crescent because we would always give them an arse kicking which would often turn into a deadly game without frontiers. I always remember Paul Woodhouse slapping me dead hard across my head and it nearly sent me into next week with the sheer brute force of his hand. I got him back though by scoring the winner of this enthralling game by chipping the ball over Paul Hanratty's outstretched fingers. We would play football morning, noon and night and the hostilities would only cease at the final whistle. At the end of proceedings we would shake hands with each other and then go back to being best mates again. Even though my ears would still be ringing off that premeditated slap, I would put it to one side and just took it as part and parcel of my many scrapes in the world of football!

We got on really well with the Crescent and we would join forces with them to fight our enemy who were the 'four squares'. These violent altercations would always end up with lots of casualties on both sides and we really did not take any prisoners in our quest for supremacy. This barren piece of land was a no go area for us and we classed their impoverished folk as the poor relations of our own grand empire. I still have a scar on my forehead from such battles which were fought out on neutral ground known as the 'ollar'. The 'ollar' was a great setting for battle because of its proximity and it was also a haven for sticks and stones that really did break your bones. While entrenched on the battlefield with my 'catty' I peered over some rocks when I copped for one right on my bloody fod. I seem to recall that my workaholic dad was not best pleased with me and he called me a "Nincompoop" or something to that effect because he was on his way to work. He missed the bus whilst attending to my gashed forehead and he used his knotted white hanky to stem the crimson flow of blood. For my troubles, he pulled my sideboards dead hard and sent this battle wearied soldier back to his barracks. This just added insult to my already injured and aching head as I trundled off up the stairs and into my own readymade royal infirmary!

The only time we ever fell out with the Crescent was when it came to that time of the year when we all loved to hate each other and that time of the year was of course November 5th. The lead up to bommie night itself was always a period of time that would be greeted with great anticipation. All of the kids and adults alike would battle it out as we fought to outdo each other on our explosive night of glorious colour and warmth. Bonfire night was always a massive celebration for us all and saw the biggest fires in Liverpool city centre since the depressing days of the 'blitzkrieg'. We would match these out of order bombing raids which were ruthlessly dished out by them bastard German fellahs. For weeks leading up to the big night, we would all go collecting bommie wood in every nook and cranny that we could plunder and pillage for absolutely miles around. If it was not nailed down then it would become the fodder to feed our massive 'wicker man' bonfires. They were easily the biggest fires in town and we were never bothered by the fire brigade because we would just tell them where to go.

I remember one year when the firemen went on strike and the city centre was full of 'green goddesses' which were the army pretenders for the real thing. I could piss further than these water gun machines because they would struggle to put out a candle or even a sparkler for that matter. We robbed a big old fashioned rail cart from Lime street station to make sure that we had all the transport that we would require to shift our masses of wood. This trolley carried all of the wood that we would somehow find in abundance on our many 'cloak and dagger' raids of the vast wooded land in our midst. This land contained absolutely no trees whatsoever but it was full of empty warehouses that stood in dereliction and gave us all the wood that we ever needed. We would collect wood all day and night and then we would have to stash it somewhere safe so that the crescent could not rob it off us. The 'would be' pyre was also guarded day and night in varying shifts that would change personnel every couple of hours to keep the Vikings of the Crescent firmly at bay. Sometimes we would get had over and it really did cause trouble but we would wreak our revenge by taking back what was rightfully ours. We would carry out these raids at dusk or dawn and we would take a little bit more just for good measure. This was to let the Crescent know that we were not going to be outdone on our special night but I am sure that the likes of Mike Tallon or Paul Birchall would say otherwise. These two little villains have been a great help to me lately and they have totally inspired me to take this book to the highest level of integrity, so thanks guys!

It was our night of extreme colour and excitement as the rainbow fountains and Catherine wheels would explode to light up the smoke filled skies. The whistling from the rockets gave out a deafening screech that would envelop the black skies above us and echo into the cosy flames of our raging inferno. I remember one night when Marie Lindsay set a rocket off from her veranda on the 'Vicky' and it went straight through a window on transport house. Poor Marie was mortified but all of the kids just revelled in it because it was both spectacular and dead funny in its comic capers kind of way. The flames would lick the night sky and leave us with an intimate glow as we threw our spuds on to the fire and feasted away until the early hours of the bleak wintry morning. The morning smog would see us resume our peace with the Crescent and again we would join forces with our allies. We would meet in no man's land to take up arms and together we would obliterate the four squares because we were bored. We would resume our hostilities with them and we would wage our campaign of terror, on to the unsuspecting enemy with a renewed vigour!

It was also a time of rich pickings for me and my sidekick 'Jenko' because we would go on the guy outside the 'Byrom' pub or to the more affluent and well heeled 'Sportsman'. The latter was in the big precinct in town and we cleaned up with a guy that none of the revellers had ever seen before. The mega money was made in and around the local boozers of town because of the absolute legend that was to become known as my type of guy for a very long and profitable time. The guy in question who would be at my side on my many jaunts into town was known as the eccentric and quite shocking 'Dick RedHead'! He was in fact a dummy and a real ventriloquist's dream that served me very well for many years to come because he was a real money spinner for me and 'Jenko'. He got his name because of his shocking tufts of red hair that were incorporated on to his head rather skilfully and he turned out to be a real character in his own right. Dick was evidently a dummy of reputable gains and he was definitely a character of notable worth due to the fact that he was a not so living legend. With his black plastic boots and his black and white checked suit he was a real dapper and his voice box was in perfect working order. I practised my 'Norman Wisdom' routine in front of a mirror that told me many a time, that I was pretty shit at my London palladium efforts. He would go on to be a firm family favourite because I got him as a present for Christmas and he eventually became a part of me and my limited but well delivered one line "gottle a geer" act. The real name of this dummy was in fact Mr. Parlanchin and he originated from Spain so if anybody has one of these 'Chucky's' knocking around in your loft then please let me know and I will make you a decent offer. I do not care how much you ask for this dummy because I will just sit outside The Lord Warden with him on bommie night and cadge off the punters until I get my money reimbursed tenfold!

I worked very hard to hone my skills as a ventriloquist and I practised every day and night in my bedroom. I soon perfected my act on the many nights that I would need him to double up as my 'sugar daddy' and he made this budding star an absolute mint. I was always very enterprising and always had my own few bob which I mostly earned from an honest day's work. I had various jobs that I did around my commune and refreshingly, they were of the legal kind. Having my own few bob was imperative so I could afford to buy my 'mighty atoms' and my 'Roman candles' along with my packets of not so entertaining 'Sparklers'. Most of my 'thunderclap' bangers were damp squibs and frustratingly I would never get the desired effect. I would just snap these duds in half and carefully gather up the gunpowder into a pile that was destined to become my magic 'genie'. Here I was, completely losing the plot like that blow up merchant 'Guy Fawkes' and I lost count of the many times that my genie act would go wrong. I would be left sitting there in a cloud of black acrid smoke as the plumes and fumes of my detonation would make me cough and splutter. The result would see me with no eyelashes or eyebrows and a face that was as black as a chimney sweep but oh so cute in a weird and wonderful way. If we could not get fireworks then we would improvise by making our own bombs out of pilot matches and a piece of silver foil. We would assemble these little 'fizzers' ourselves and we would then lodge them into the brickwork of the tenements to be set off. Safety was never an issue with these replica fireworks but they would still achieve their guided aim to simply appease us. After the flames had extinguished themselves, the tarmac in the middle of the square would just be a melted mass of cinders and bed springs. They would litter the massive crater which housed our bonfire along with everything else from door fittings to cabinet handles.

The bombsite would remain intact until the council decided to clean it up and if we were lucky then they would re-tarmac the surface again. Our football pitch would be restored back to its former glory and the old rail cart would begin a new lease of life as a massive thrill seeking go-kart. The wooden trolley with the big metal wheels would be used as a form of transport for all the kids to hurtle down Hunter Street. On one occasion we travelled down the more fitting 'backie' which was the piece of land that stood between the Gardens and the Crescent. Barry Healy was the master of ceremonies and we were bombing down the 'backie' with about 100 kids on board when Barry lost control of the situation. We promptly smashed straight in to the solid wall which sent us all flying in many different and very painful directions. The majority of us ended up on the floor like scatter cushions and poor Barry broke his leg for his troubles. His dad Billy then took our omnibus apart in a frenzied attack with a gleaming and scary looking battle axe. It has been said that the wheels off this massive beetle buggy were kept on Barry's veranda as some kind of ornament but poor Barry must have painfully cringed at the very sight of them.

The little mound affectionately known as the 'backie' kept us all at arm's length in times of open warfare which was thankfully very seldom and was never really that serious in its conviction. We saved our ranking inhibitions for the four squares as we continued the 'struggle' that would rear its ugly head from time to time and we had to be on our guard at all times. They were sly but never really all that cunning and we picked them off easily with the minimum of fuss. These scoundrels always seemed to be in awe of us and our forever growing notoriety but they never once got the upper hand in our clashes. They succumbed to our 'might' and never really fitted in to my way of thinking or for that matter, my sense of childhood logic.

Whenever I needed to go to Soho Street I did so very sheepishly and I would often travel under the cover of relative darkness. Sometimes, I would take refuge under my ma's camel coloured duffle coat which offered me a safe passage through the subway and past the clutches of these un-liberated immigrants. I only tolerated the place because it was home to 'Austin's chippy' and a vast array of inviting sweet shops that sold the delights of 'Spanish gold' or the other little precious gems that were called 'Golden nuggets'! These little bags of glistening chewies were great and the durable bag that they were dispensed in would transform itself into a pretty decent wallet. Soho Street was also a place where my aunty Peggy Shields lived with her husband Pauly in Jenkinson Walk. They were always surrounded by their loving family who meant the world to them and I spent many happy hours with all of them, in their home. Peggy was a lovely serene woman and Pauly always kept us entertained with his love of playing the spoons like the seasoned pro that he was. A little further on was a block of flats that were depressingly called the 'Piggeries' and my lovely aunty Marie lived there with her 'top' husband Vinnie. The rest of the crew took 'Murphy's law' on board and together they lived in perfect harmony amongst these Wuthering Heights. I loved going there because I would get to play with all the girls' toys which I found odd at the time but my 3 cousins were girls so what could I do? The 3 little bears in question were sisters Marie, Denise and baby Collette!

All of the money that I earned on my many happy adventures was wisely saved up and soon my wallet outgrew itself. I steadily progressed with my business acumen and I moved on to a 'Rover tin' that was kept safely under the confines of my bed. This vault of sorts incorporated my smelly socks that would be employed menacingly to ward off any would be 'tea leaves'. My sense of security was never broken and in time my little nest egg became a colossal amount. That same Rover tin went on to house thousands of ladybirds that had descended on our square in a biblical swarm that was to reach every room in our small but very tidy flat. I got grounded for ten minutes and was then allowed out to continue with my acts of Botany in the safe haven of the ever dependable St. Johns Gardens. I loved these gardens and the area that surrounded it which in itself offered a plentiful supply of nature to add to my wildlife days on expedition. I would collect all manner of insects on my travels including caterpillars or grasshoppers and on the odd occasion maybe a daddy long legs. I would often find these lanky legged creatures in the sandy joints of our immense facade and I have to admit that I did pull their legs off randomly.

I always remember when the bin strike was on and the 'ollar' represented what could only be described as a makeshift tip that was pretty disgusting at the time. This heap of shit was crawling with vermin but it also offered me the delights of muck turning into brass. I would come across all kinds of crap that I could utilise and maybe make a few bob on. Amongst the shit and dirty linen would be ointments and tablets or even used 'jam rags' but the main thing that I would be searching for would be aerosols. These little detonators were great and they always added a boom to the many fires that we would lovingly tend to in all four corners of the square. The bin strike also gave us a breed of insect that I definitely would not collect because it was the vile and grotesque looking cockroach. These monstrosities always scared the shit out of me and they scurried across the many mountains of rotting rubbish like miniature tanks. I avoided these beetles like the plague because I was only into ladybirds at the time and cockroaches had no place in my ever growing collection of insects. Rats were also prevalent at this depressing time but instead of scaring me, I warmed to them because of a rat called 'Ben' in the brilliant film that was called 'Rats'. This film was terrifying but I cried my eyes out at the end when poor little Ben died and then that great song was played out to the credits!

Every kid in this vast complex paraded as mates with each other and if you fell out with one kid then you would literally have another 100 kids to choose from. Finding mates was always dead easy for me and I had lots of good mates in my far reaching days of socialism. Each kid that I crossed paths with would be checked out for potential and vetted before I opened negotiations as to what kind of benefits they could offer me. If they had a bike or an 'Atari' games console then I would be their 'bestest' mate forever and ever. This mutual friendship would normally last for a couple of days because familiarity breeds contempt and especially if I had punctured their tyres or beat them at 'spacies'. It was really that simple and it made every other day a little more different from the last one. My liberating days would always give me something variable to look forward to because I never knew what was going to happen from one day to the next. Real love was all around me and I prospered well along this path of life where happiness was conceived in every imaginable way. I foraged around and found a world full of entertainment that was always waiting for me to grace its stage and this stage was in my mind. One minute I was just a normal kid doing my rounds and the next minute I would be on a raft and playing out the part of Robinson Crusoe!

When our parents would choose go out on the ale, we would take it in turns as to whose house we would sit-off in. We gorged ourselves on a childhood of rebellion that was awash with packets of Smiths 'salt 'n shake' crisps and bottles of lemonade that were dispensed from a very 70s soda stream. We would listen to 'Showaddywaddy' and drink stewed tea from a teapot that would be left to warm up on the eternal flame that was the pilot light on the old cookers. This was positioned at the centre of these old fashioned gas appliances and its heat just took the edge off what was to be a half decent cup of tea. We used any means possible to enjoy the finer things in life like 'Mantunna' tea and 'Mothers pride' toast but there would always be a fight over who would get the elusive crust of bread. I would always plant the crust and I often found them months later in an LP cover or even under my pillow in a sorry state of fine mouldy bread crumbs. If there was only one crust left then we would do a 'beaneo' and there would always be murder amongst best friends in order to acquire it. No one ever ended up brown bread as a result of these minor 'nudger' disagreements but there would always be a slice of mayhem. I would somehow always appear victorious when it came to fighting for the crust and it was just another accolade for me to go with all the rest. My fight for survival was paramount and I needed to be at the top of my game because my counterparts were developing their own school of thoughts. The floodlit square was a safe haven for us and doors were genuinely left wide open as there was no need for security in these times of utter wellbeing?

This self-imposed illusion was finally shattered on a night of heartbreak and shame with the shocking murder of a beautiful and angelic cherub called 'Simon Gouldson'. I do not wish to upset Simon's family by dwelling on this catastrophe for them and one that sent shockwaves through the very foundations of this now labelled 'unsafe' haven. I will keep this story very short but I feel as though it should be logged in Simon's memory. I have remained very close to his loving family over the years and they have continued to be my friends throughout my impending years away from these now, very tainted gardens. The murder shook the community and the decent people who once lived a carefree lifestyle now grieved in sheer disbelief and horror. It really did put things into perspective and it would trouble every single person in the community and change the face of my beloved home forever. Worse still was to be the effect that it would have on this innocent child's bereft family and everyone's sympathy would never be enough. Simon's grandmother was the very lady who had helped bring me into this world and it really was heartbreaking for everyone concerned at this most depressing of times. I really felt compelled to get this in because I loved this kid so much and I would often push him around in a big old fashioned pram for hours on end. Simon would just giggle away in his own little happy world of adventure and I often think about him and his brothers Jay, Scott and John who was also Simon's twin brother. I would just like to thank every member of his family and of course Simon himself for giving me my own cherished memories of a beautiful and innocent kid from the block. Simon's lovely family have given me their blessing to include this sad story and it serves me as a platform to offer my own personal tribute to such a wonderful child. He broke my heart and everybody else's who knew and loved him because he really was idolised by everyone. I would just like to a finish off this paragraph with a little but poignant tribute to baby 'Simon Gouldson' who was 'our little angel' and who will never ever be forgotten. "Rest in peace beautiful boy".

There was always something entertaining happening in every corner of the square which would normally involve a domestic fight or a simple game of 'kerby'. There would always be a gang of girls singing with their skirts pulled up over their heads and this was pretty handy for the rampant lads. We would always be on the prowl to cop a quick clock of their 'skimps' which often entailed in us getting an almighty slap across the face. The girls would invariably tuck their kilts into their knickers as they played hopscotch or 'two ball' or whatever for that matter. They would juggle with two baldy tennis balls for hours on end and they did the knickers trick accordingly. My indiscretions cost me dearly but I was only being a lad because that's what lads do!

I had always wished that my red blood would turn blue for obvious reasons because I am a proud Evertonian through and through. That would not always be the case though as you will soon find out in a tale that will compound me in horror and shame forever. I will tell you my very own story of a 'poor boy' who was the scouser Bobby and I was sent far away from my home to repent my unforgiveable sins. I will reveal all soon about my other minor indiscretion but it's a sore point and one that still haunts me to this day. Let me get back to the other things that went on in our now embellished 'violent playground' and I will return to the above story after I have had a bottle of mentholated spirits. I am going to need a little bit of Dutch courage to get me through that particular story and I do not mean that cheesy kind of double Dutch?

The sight of two dogs bonking around the square without a care in the world would not seem out of place and they were often of the same sex. This was very strange to me but also very funny at the time and I am just glad that I kept my distance from 'Fellah Sedgewick'! The dogs of the day commanded their very own meaning of self importance and were given their own status symbols with names like, 'Fellah Sedgewick', 'Rocky Parry', 'Kim Jenkins', 'Sooty O ' Rourke' and the late but great ' Fritz Miello'! They would all take it in turns to shaft poor 'Snowy Robbo' and thus leaving her demented owner 'Mary Robbo' to bring up the scores of pups that popped out in all different shapes and sizes. Many were the days that you would see poor Mary knocking at all of the usual 'suspect's' doors as she would point the finger and demand family allowance or compensation for her new breed of mutts. The pups would all strike an uncanny resemblance to all of the possible fathers in question who in panic just ran away to plant their puppy making seeds elsewhere. The same could not be said for poor 'Fellah' though because he electrocuted his own furry balls when he had a piss on a lamp post. He inadvertently sent his little fluffy bag to kingdom come in a puff of smoke that completely destroyed his doghood and resigned him to a life of lamp post phobia!

Mary was a true legend in herself and she was very kind to all of the kids around the square who in return loved her so much but we would sometimes taunt her with games like knock and run. We would also pull her bog chain through the open toilet window which was a trait that was practised on nearly every landing. Another misdemeanour would be to place a bottle on her wall with a piece of cotton attached to her door knocker. We would then knock on her door and when she would open it, we would be hiding on the landings silently sniggering and waiting for the resulting smash. Anyway, the bottle would crash to the floor to the screams of "I'm telling your mothers you little bleeders"------ "I know where you all live" or words to that effect. She

57

truly was a lovely woman who only passed away a few months ago at the grand old age of 97 years. She lived out her final days in a nursing home that was not far away from where she had once lived and prospered herself at one great time or another. I visited Mary last year and it was a great experience to actually see this woman at all. The legend that she was will always shine on as she now rests, forever in our hearts!

Most of my memories have rushed back to me in an instant and left me feeling great as I have planted the seeds that will continue to grow in what remains of this epic tabloid. The joy of writing this book now takes me on to a reunion party that was organised by me and my good friend Christine Hanratty. We held the big night in the Sylvestrian club in Vauxhall on October 30th 2009 and it truly was a night to remember for all the right reasons. The night was a sell out and went on to be one of the best nights out that the 'Gardenite's' had enjoyed for years and it brought this great community back together again. The entertainment was supplied by old boys Gerard Fagan (*In A City Living*) and Paul Sudbury (*Gardens of Stone*) who both fronted a band called wait for it------- 'The Gardens'! They were absolutely brilliant to say the least and hopefully they will make it to my own impending and long awaited book launch at the Liner Hotel in Lime Street. I would like to thank Gerard Fagan for his support in me writing this book with his useful and encouraging words of wisdom and I would also like to thank all of you for inspiring me to finally get my fascinating tales to print. Also on stage that night was local historian and my old mate Frank Carlyle who gave us a history lesson not to be forgotten. Frank was also born in this rich pool of talent that was Gerard Gardens and I know how proud he is of our empire because I can feel it every time I speak to him. This doctorate of a man has been invited to do the foreword in this book and gratefully he has accepted my offer. I am very pleased with that but I don't know what he will write about my book, so we will leave that one for now. I must also mention the 'old time crooner' and the all round entertainer better known as Jimmy Hackett. This great showman belted out some great tunes himself and he added to the authenticity of the night as did the excellent band 'Jonville'!

The evening was capped off by me singing a song that I wrote for Gerard Gardens and my set also included the nostalgic anthems of Como's 'And I love you so' and a fitting if not masterful rendition of 'For the good times'. The latter song was sung from the heart and it captivated everyone with its poignancy. It brought tears of pride to my mother's eyes as she and her little boy revelled in the fact that he had brought everyone together on this never to be repeated night of sheer brilliance. The event was captured in all its glory by Liverpool's finest photographer to date and my mate, Gerard Fleming. Gerard has kindly offered to do the cover of my book for me and I feel as though I am in really good company. I proudly accepted this offer from a true gardens ambassador and I have seen some samples of his great work so I am very confident that he will produce an absolute masterpiece. The cover of the book is a sketch that Joe O 'Connnell did for me ten years ago and it has shamefully been gathering dust on top of my wardrobe ever since. The brilliant sketch now has pride of place on my living room wall and it has been framed with total gratitude. I suppose it is fate really because Joe is my uncle Danny's brother and I thank him so much for kindly giving me permission to use this fantastic picture. The whole book is littered with intimacy and this intimacy makes it all the more rewarding because everyone who has had a part to play, has played it majestically!

Gerard Fleming was also a dweller of Gerard Gardens and he lived in one of the most famous addresses in Liverpool at the time. I guess that he has also got some great stories to tell you but you will have to wait for his own book of magic to see his evident worth as a top lens man. His pictures completely freak me out because you feel as though you are there and I really hope that his own masterpiece is not that far away. The epicentre of this social activity was number 56 Christian Street and was situated more or less facing our veranda. It was home of the notorious 'Pontack' public house and it was run by the great Peggy Gaskill. She served the community so well for years with a sense of vigour and an authority that was stamped on to this intimate and very happy setting. Peggy offered her own personal charm and warm welcomes to everyone who would happen to venture in there on any given night. Her warmth was so often displayed at the many social gatherings that took place over the years and indeed every night of the week but especially at the weekends. She was also the mother of my mate and that guy who is responsible for doing my book cover so thank you very much Gerard because the end result will be my crowning glory. My nana Shields would often drink in this watering hole with the likes of Jane (golden) Goulding, Martha Strode, Maggie Moore, Kate McGuiness and of course Annie Tallon who amongst many others had the pleasure of knowing her. They all partied together whilst playing their own part in my nana's life by being one of her so solid bingo crew!

In later years this famous pub changed hands and it was my uncle Charlie Pepper and his wife Joan who were now at the helm. The community was fading fast and it became a bit of a struggle for everyone concerned but they employed their own goodwill on everyone and it was fondly returned on numerous occasions. Young Charlie got the place rocking again with Al Jolson and our Jacqueline also shared the limelight with her lovely renditions of timeless lullabies. Gary also added to the array of talent on show with his great impersonations of Bruce Forstyh and the likes. My personal favourite mimic though has to be the magical 'Rigsby' routine that Gary had off to a tee and he would always have everyone in stitches when he performed it. Our poor Daniel was left waiting in the wings but he had attracted notoriety upon himself as a real life miracle baby. It was a big deal at the time because it had made the headlines in the *Liverpool Echo* so he had already made his claim to fame. They strived to keep the community together and made a real good go of the 'Pontack' but they were fighting a losing battle as the area became a building site for demolition. People got fed up with the dereliction that ensued and moved away to pastures a little more greener. The 'Pontack' has now been refurbished but it is pretty vacant and if I sell enough of these books then I will resurrect the old place along with all the spirits that were served in this celebrated little hub. I will move on now as I will tell you a little more about the blast from the past that was of course our reunion night and I even got my picture taken with Paul Birchall!

Here I was conducting this fabulous night in a blaze of publicity and glory as we were giving everybody present at this occasion a night that will live on with them forever. Their hearts and souls were on parade and it really was just mad for me to be actually witnessing all of these old faces on one historic night. Many legends of the day were put there right before my very own disbelieving eyes and I was completely awestruck. A gang of pure 'salt of the earth' people who had heralded from my never dodgy past were lapping it up and they were having the time of their lives. This social gathering was all about everyone just catching up with each other after spending over 30 years apart in some cases. The natives of Liverpool 3 were left clambering for tickets to this most memorable of events to date and to say that I was as proud as punch would be an understatement to say the least. I had actually pulled this night off and it was my baby and a massive thrill to finally stamp my own mark on to what is genuinely termed as folklore. The night was to be tinged with sadness though as words that I used to my mother would come back to haunt me and leave me feeling so desperately sad and despondent. At the end of the night, I was dancing with my mother who looked as divine as ever and so in her element as I whispered the fateful words "look around you mum and look at all the smiling faces" she smiled as I continued "a few of the old timers present may not be here if I do another reunion night next year" She nodded accordingly as she danced the night away and the most heartbreaking thing about my words that night were that she ultimately was the first person to leave us. The night remains bitter sweet for me for obvious reasons but I am really glad that I did it because at least me ma had time to meet up with all of her old friends and many acquaintances. I suppose that she was just saying goodbye to everyone and this notion gives me immense comfort. Since that great night, I been asked to do another but I sadly declined the offer with a heavy heart because it would not really be a reunion night if my mother was not there. I am afraid that you heard it here first folks and I am really sorry but there is no point in me putting a brave face on for one night only. I would basically just be going through the motions and I would not take it on again if my heart was not fully in it, but never say never again...innit!

I will now continue my journey with more stories that helped shape my life as I got older but probably not much wiser. As the years passed by, I would use everything that I had learned along the way to put me in good stead and I was a really independent kid because of this. I carried on with these learning curves all the way through my childhood and immersed them into my teens and right up to the present day. The older I got then the more chances I would take and when I was just seven years old I broke my leg not once but twice in quick succession. Both breaks were very painful indeed but I soldiered on like the trooper that I had become. For some unexplained reason I used to love dropping off high walls and the higher the wall then the better the fall, or so I stupidly thought until one fateful day. This painful day gave way to another crude nick name for me to add to the already long list of nick names that I had already accrued. I would deem these cruel jibes as bad skits because the taunts would often reduce me to tears in their deliverance. My tears turned into a river of sorrows when I quickly realised that I could not stand up and run away from my fall of grace. I dropped off a wall in Gerard Crescent and landed on the corner of a big concrete step which basically snapped my leg in two. This escapade resulted in me getting plastered for the second time in my short life. The first time was in Paris and on my jaunt of debauchery that took me away from such cruel taunts! Poor Jimmy (golden) Gouldson was the unfortunate ambulance driver on this mercy dash because I smothered him in plaster from head to toe. I totally whitewashed his four door saloon and left a trail of chalk right up to my front door. I will be forever grateful to Jimmy and also his loving family for a great number of reasons and I will be waiting for a pint off Jay or Scott on my launch night. If they buy a book off me, I will get them one back for old time's sake but I will be sending our Franky to the bar!

Bobby, plaster and finally Paris seemed to go together well and the trick of snapping my bones was to be repeated just days after my leg had healed from my first calamity. On this occasion our Lorraine was the main culprit and my days of pain would be compounded for the foreseeable future. She took on the role of Sterling Moss of all people

62

but she drove like a typical woman and for that reason only, I will liken her to Kate Moss instead. The little 'Mare Ellen' was pushing me around in one of the very versatile prams that I mentioned earlier on in the plot and she was going way too fast. She tore around the gardens aimlessly and was a bit like the Tasmanian devil if I am to be perfectly honest! As I put my already bad leg down to utilise my brakes, she promptly ran over it and that was that for me. There I was once more like that bluff 'Steve Austin' lying on the floor in agony and waiting for the doctors to rebuild me once again! These big bone breaking prams really were chariots of fire that would often be taken apart by me with my pilfered spanners. The wheels would be randomly removed and then hammered on to a plank of wood and so my go-kart would be complete. Unfortunately I was going nowhere fast or should I say that my journey was going nowhere painfully slow. I was shuttled about like a Roman emperor in my battle weary carriage but I was eager to get back to my days of being a gladiator. In the most severe cases, if I did not have a carriage man then I would be going painfully nowhere at all and that was not good for me because I was a foot soldier. I could not make my thunderbird go-kart yet because I needed this blag- leather pram for the far more pressing engagements of my ongoing disability!

I was like an Airfix model with so many parts of me either missing or broken. The journey back to hospital had a touch of déjà vu about it but something or someone was missing. Oh yes, Jimmy Goulding! I made my way back to the ward and I waited impatiently as I gazed at the cartoon characters that were displayed on all four walls of this casualty gaff. All of the nurses knew me by my first name and I am sure that I have still got some of their telephone numbers in my little red book. I would be a little bit scared to ring them though because they would be about 83 years old now and that nurse's uniform would not look the same somehow. I was in and out of hospital all the time for all manner of things and some of my escapades were pretty embarrassing. One such memory would be the time when I did my Tommy Cooper routine for a laugh and just like his many dodgy array of tricks my efforts also backfired. By royal command the trick involved putting a bead down one ear and it supposedly coming out of the other one. It just ended up getting firmly lodged right down my wax worked ear drum and it was off to hospital for me again. After much fiddling about, the doctor finally prised it out of my lug hole "Just like that" and then I was on my merry way. Another trip to the infirmary was required by me when me and Kevin Sedgewick decided to settle our differences by way of a real life dual. We met in the square and battled ferociously with our impromptu swords that were made out of hard plastic. Kevin caught me with a corker right above my left eye and I was summoned to hospital once more with a gaping wound. I was patched up again and I still bear the scars today but instead of being angry at Kevin, I am eternally grateful to him because that scar made me look hard and it was definitely a hit with the girls.

Getting back to my broken leg and carrying on now where I left off as our Lorraine ran over to Barney's to summon my overworked mother for help. My poor mother was in bits to see her little cherub also reduced to bits in a broken and undignified stupor. I was literally lying in a crumpled heap underneath the 'Vicky' and my snorkel coat was my only means of support. I was crying out in pain and also smiling in the safe knowledge that I would be spending another six weeks in my glorified stagecoach. This ramshackle of a pram was needed once again and was now to become like my second home. I spent the whole of the summer holidays in that miniature caravan and everyone would take it in turns to push me around the squares and through the arches.

I was never one to be grounded and just because my life was now on wheels, it did not stop my ever growing thirst for adventure. No matter what hindrance was put before me, I just took it on the chin or in my case I took it on the shin and shuffled on aimlessly. I did not have a stride anymore but I went on to star in our Lorraine's communion celebrations and I used my impediment to my great advantage. I went on to make an absolute fortune that day and this was due to my state of health and the prolonged jaunt of my un-wellbeing. I reckon that I got well more money than our Biddy on the day but I also guessed that she would probably have me off for my ill gotten gains when we got back home. Life was far too valuable to waste I thought and I would never let a single day pass by without there being some kind of commotion going on. I would invariably be in the thick of it as per usual but I would not have wanted it to be any other way at all! Life was just a game to me and I played hard for my reward but I took the chances to earn it. I took the rough with the smooth and this smooth operator went on to be a really rough diamond of notable attributes. These words are not accolades of course and I am not throwing bouquets at myself because as I have said throughout this book, it is an adventure story and I just happen to be the star!

My days of being stuck in a pram were definitely a sympathy grabber and I utilised all of my finely immobilised skills to gain a healthy advantage on my long road to recovery. I would gingerly take my time to get around in my 'spaz' chariot and it was a good time for the attention that I steadily sought to be unleashed. I would be the benefactor of dozens of super-balls, sweets, comics and all manner of things including the old 'tanners' which I gladly collected and saved up for any number of rainy days. My old friend Francis Wiles would always walk along our landing having been to the 'Pontack' for a few scoops and he would always give me a couple of bob. He would give me a handful of slummy and I would be scanning the pile for silver because copper was always too heavy. I counted out my pennies and shillings while Francis threw a song in for good measure and then went home to the cremated remains of his roast dinner. I was friends with his son Steven Wiles and they in turn were friends of my ever extended family that also included his lovely mother Cathleen.

Dominic Butcher would always pass by and sing out the words "Jay-Joe-jeans and his dolly beans" which to this day I still do not know where they came from or what they meant. It always made me smile though and Dominic was one of the many great characters who filled my life with laughter. By fate my son was to be called Jay and I used this very ditty to embarrass him when he was just a nipper. He would go ballistic when we all sang it to him but he now takes it as an accolade of affection which I think is great because of its origins. Dominic lived with my dad's workmate and his brother Peter who was also the brother of my mate and great neighbour Christie 'Boots' Butcher. These three wise men were always good to me and they were always the perfect next door neighbours in this land of living legends. It's funny how little things like this stay in your memory and fill you with a sense of warmth that you carry on with you through your life and then pass them down to the younger generation. This gives our own kids the chance to grasp what all the fuss was really about and it keeps our own memories well and truly alive. This is another reason why I chose to write this book because I want to educate our offspring on the place that I and many others still hold up in a very high regard. Our Jay has already taken an interest in what I am writing and he is really intrigued by the furore that it is incorporating even before its release. I must admit that I am really having a ball on my rounds of literary conquests and I cannot wait for the reaction to my book!

When I got back on to my feet, my earning power steadily increased and it improved dramatically as a result. I genuinely started off my own business when I was just seven years old and I would give any apprentice or self styled entrepreneur a run for their money. My dad had a sideline or two along with his other nightmare of a job in Otis elevators and they also served me well to earn a few extra bob in the process. He earned extra cash for the pot by selling fresh meat from our home and people from all over the square were his customers. Soon they would become my customers too for a lean cut of the profits that were always open to negotiation. I held down a steady job which would include the delivery of the finest cuts of beef and endless packets of streaky bacon. We were then sent on our rounds to collect payment for the ribs and T-bone steaks that gave me arthritis in my cabbaged knees. I would ache for days on end because of the colossal weight of these mammoth joints and I am still waiting for my muscles to develop as promised by my dad. The debts would be collected every Thursday evening which was pay day for most of the inhabitants and the best time to go knocking on the doors of the many landings. We had lifts installed that never seemed to work and most of the time they just stunk of piss and rollie's. This was a shame really because I never ever saw them in working order and I just saw them as antiquated ornaments of no worth. Sadly it was a sign of the times and of the demise that would finally take a firm grip on these chosen but now very vulnerable people. Many dwellers were getting tired of the old place and they looked for a way out of the 'rat trap' that was slowly developing. The corridors of Westminster and the sheer lack of investment by the local city council soon ate away at the very foundations of our square and the end was definitely nigh for us. I blame the bastard Tory government or the shady councillors who washed their dirty hands in the very fountain that we had learned to call our own. These great tenements of prominence could have been saved and refurbished just like they did with the old 'Bullring' of St. Andrews Gardens. Like the famous 'Cavern', our days would become very numbered and we were littered with an overpowering gloom and doom that was far from being "fab"!

Let us now go back to my days of earning a crust and replenishing anything that most people would happily have thrown away but not me. I would turn anything that was deemed shit into something worthy that I could probably sell on to my many satisfied customers. There were many takers as I affectionately seem to remember and I was just happy to explore every avenue that was made available to me. It was another opportunity for me to gain yet more valuable experience as I now had all the tools of the trade that were required by my vast efforts. I utilised every single one of these attributes to my advantage and I was very close to being the finished article. It was very hard work being me but also very rewarding because on top of our wages of ten bob a week I had the chance to earn just that little bit more. We could and we would easily double that amount of money with the generosity that was shown by our loyal and benevolent customers. They appreciated what we did for them and they kindly rewarded the service that we provided for them, in their quest for good quality chops. I would always put our kid and our Lorraine on to bum steers in order for me to pick up the biggest tipsters and it worked a treat for me. They were not best pleased with me when they realised that they were being hoodwinked but I carried on regardless and very much to their utter dismay. They have got their own version of events and it was probably them who had put me on to an inglorious trail of fruitless endeavour. My biggest tipster by far had to be a lady called Mary Mac and she was a lovely woman who was kind to all of the kids who would cross her path. I was always happy being Bobby but more importantly I was a 'real gone kid' with an insatiable thirst for wealth and I went on to be a self-made hundreds-of-tanners-aire!

The meat was always delivered in a big blue van by a large and imposing man called Dennis Campbell and I reckon that he had done a few pies or legs of lamb in his time as a butcher. He and my dad ran a very lucrative little business right on their very own doorstep and I learned a lot from my dad in that respect for which I am eternally grateful. Pay day would always see me running over to Barneys or to the mobile van and my wages would take a severe battering. On my return I would lock myself in my bedroom and I would shut off from the outside world so I could feast alone. I would marvel at my W*hizzer and chips* or my trusted *Beano* comics that I loved to read and life on the block was seemingly fine and dandy. After gorging myself with the fruit and nuts of my labour I would then go into the kitchen and settle myself down to watch our black and white television set. It was manufactured by the pioneers of their day Grundig and it gave me pleasures abound as I watched everything from Double Decker with that doughnut geezer to the fabulous extremes of Love thy neighbour with Alf Garnett. I would be in complete awe of the impoverished delights of Rising damp with Leonard Rossiter playing the affable and side splitting Rigsby. Next to the telly was our Viscount music system which was a gem in its day and made us feel a little bit more posh than what we actually were. This mean set of decks was at the centre of many good times along the way and with the addition of my dad's reel to reel tape recorder we really did make sweet music. We had a very ornate but old fashioned fire surround and this hearth provided us with the hub of a very intimate setting that epitomised cosiness. It was always a pain in the arse though when we would have to get up dead early to take our delivery of coal and this freezing routine put me off coal fires for life. The lava lamp completed the setting as did the picture of that fit woman on the wall that everyone seemed to have at the time and was so randomly pointless to say the least!

Thursday was always a roast day (yes we had two) and I would leg it home from school to watch the Woody Woodpecker show and tuck into the finest cuts of beef and roasties. I feasted on a second helping of homemade apple pie before going out on a full stomach to carry out my weekly chores. I would then settle down with my mam to watch Top of the Pops and I loved this instalment of music to bits because it was a chance for me to see all of my heroes in action.

The movers and shakers of the day were of interest to me but only a couple of them really caught my eye with their over the top regalia. I was looking for a band that would take me 3 steps closer to my 'teddy boy' heaven and I found two bands that would hopefully take me there. The bands on display would be forensically tested and I would gather up any evidence that was deemed to be important to my quest. A requirement was set to either make or shake me and I opted for both as I rattled and rolled my way around the limited dance floors! I went from the innocent days of puppy love by the Osmond's to the grown up influence of bands like Showaddywaddy or The Darts and I was definitely coming of age! They were the hippest bands around and they were also the soundtrack of a life that was always spent 'under the moon of love'. Inevitably, I wanted a 'ted suit' to complete my look and I searched high and low but it never really materialised for some reason. My ensuing disappointment was levelled at Tony Gandy because he had one and he looked like 'the bee's knees' even though it was too big on him. Tony did not have the dance moves to match his suit and I would always outshine him when it really mattered in St. Joey's Disco. My pursuit of a suit was over and I had to make do with a pair of drainpipes that looked pretty cool with my crepe soled shoes. The shockingly loud pink socks were obligatory and they illuminated the dance floor as I put to practice the many moves that would rock my world. Being 'daddy cool' was great for me and at last I had found an era of music that was so in tune with my many aspirations. I graced this magical era with both feet and I took the massive steps forward to lead me into another chapter of my life!

Other bands to hit the scene of pop stardom included our very own band called Our Kid. They made their own fame on a show called New Faces and had a number of hits including "Baby don't look back", "I can't live without you" and the timeless classic "Romeo and Juliet". They were all big hits in 1976 and this boy band were part of the bubble gum scene that was so apparent around the squares at the time. The band included the very young Terry McCreath (15), Terry Baccino (15), Brian Farrell (13) and Kevin Rowan (12) respectively. Racey were also a band that were high on my agenda and they had hits themselves including "Lay your love on me" and "Some girls". Other great songs of the day included "January" by Pilot and "Mull of Kintyre" by Wings. The latter song epitomised Gerard Gardens in a nutshell with its poignant words and its haunting melodies to match. These songs were played out amongst the rattle and hum of "Tiger Feet" by Mud and "Ballroom Blitz" by The Sweet and they were all featured in the many Christmas discos that were held in Lee Jones's Club. This club would be teeming with hundreds of manic kids who would be sporting lots of tartan as they danced away to the iconic 'Shang-a-lang' by the Bay City Rollers. You had to behave in school for the whole term to get one of the coveted tickets and these tickets were like gold dust. I was forever opening the emergency exit to let 'Jenko' in because he would have been way too naughty to ever gain a legal entrance. We used this ploy many times and it got us into the Futurist picture house on Lime Street or the ever dependable 'Odeon' on London Road.

It really was a mega time for me and my friends alike as we hustled and bustled our way through the dreams that would soon become a reality in some way or another. Again my mother was so instrumental in my well being but she pulled the wool over my eyes on many more occasions and one such time was when she 'blagged' me to eat the dreaded bowl of 'Scouse'. I hated this dish with a passion but was made to eat it as she played on the very heart strings of my quest to be a real super hero. She announced to me after a much heated disagreement that I would not be 'Spiderman' or the 'Man from Atlantis' if I did not eat my bowl of 'scouse' and I was not so hungrily horrified. I believed her and I forced the vile stuff down my throat like Popeye would have done with his cans of muscle building spinach but I never did achieve my body building dreams. I often balked at the very thought of what I was force feeding myself but I managed to put some of the carrots and all of the gristle down the front of my purple and white ball stranglers. Maybe I had been scarred for life by the fact that on one occasion our Lorraine decided to give me an extra helping of this horrible dish. She was eating her bowl of stew and she decided to be sick everywhere because she was also traumatised by this slop. I seem to remember that a piece of carrot or spud shot straight into my bowl and I thought that this lapse of table manners would get me off the hook. I was buzzing with relief but my joy soon turned to pain because nobody had witnessed what I had just seen. They did not believe a single word that I said and I just had to eat this bowl of sludge or I would not get my hard earned wages. The muscles that I had been promised never ever grew and they went on to resemble knots in cotton but I took it all on the chin. I reluctantly ate humble pie and just got on with it because at least it fuelled my many burning desires. I was haunted for years by the imposing pan of 'scouse' but in time and a with a dose of counselling I grew to love it and it became an absolute favourite of mine.

Pea soup with bacon ribs was also a delight for me along with a classic dish known locally as 'macaracca'. To the purists of our native tongue 'macaracca' was simplified as macaroni but it was not of that cheesy type which I recall as being totally disgusting. It was a pleasure to be had and it was even tastier if it was served with a crusty cob that would be used to mop up the gravy. We would get these cobs from Cousins the bakers or the many Reece's outlets that were dotted around town. These master bakers were established well before the likes of Greggs or the more popular Sayers chains and I really miss going to these cake shops with my ma for the obvious reasons. It was way before the likes of 'Sayers' had even discovered the notion of baking a cake never mind a 'tiger's tail' or a floury 'hedgehog' bloomer.

Other delicacies of this tempestuous era included 'dripping or sugar butties', 'pigs tails/feet', 'ox tongue', 'tripe' and of course the culinary delights of Johnnie Gianelli. This master of potato was the true master of his trade and the best chipster in town for miles around. He would grace and serve the hungry hub that trawled these communities and everyone would look forward to his fish, chips and mushy peas. They would be served up in the pages of the previous night's *Liverpool Echo* and the old news would give you something to read on your way home. The fine print just added to the authenticity of this chip shop and the big marble counter served me well on so many occasions of self-indulgence. It was a true establishment that would leave this great eatery lying in folklore for all of eternity because of its notoriety. This revered chip shop was so iconic and it was richly deserving of its status because it had a history that was steeped in its own greasy tradition. My uncle Joey Shields bought the giant fish plate that was displayed in the big glass window and my cousin Kayo is now the proud owner of this great gardens artefact. Our great chippy bestowed a massive honour upon itself and it went on to become a phenomenon of Gerard Gardens and the surrounding area.

Our many relatives from Peterborough would travel up north and they would sample our very northern brand of life in the fast lane. They loved their down to earth visits and we always looked forward to seeing each other because we wanted to do our bit to close the North and South divide. We were always trying to understand each other's dialect and we got it wrong at times but we would always get there in the end and we managed to communicate accordingly. Despite our social differences we were one big happy family and that special bond would never ever be broken. You all know who you are and you are all very much part of this book even if I have not mentioned you by name. Diamonds are forever because they never fade or lose their worth and their purity is mirrored by my own great memories of every single one of you. I will now return to my 'new apprentice' days with more tall stories that shook the world of finance and beyond!

Part of my business acumen was to be the official messenger to most of the residents in the Gardens and in time I branched out to run errands for the 'rezzies' of the Crescent too. The mobile van had gone from the Gardens and was now situated in the Crescent where it was owned by the Miller family. It was at the very heart of the community and served us well as it housed all the necessities that the natives of this island would need to survive. My aunties and uncles lived there and both sets of grandparents so it was pretty much rich pickings for me and this just added to what was to become my own personal empire. I had left my pilfering days behind me for good because I had moved on to bigger and better things in order to afford the right to buy my own much needed commodities.

My enterprising ways would see me knock on everybody's door to ask them if they wanted any messages doing and before no time I had built up a very profitable round. This pushed my wages up to around three quid a week which in those days was brewsters and it just paved the way for me to enjoy my life and reward those closest to me with maybe a bunch of flowers or a box of Quality Street. This showed my gentler side and was just my way of saying thank you for the life that I was now becoming accustomed to. I would not let anyone slip through the net and every message was an opening for me to make a tidy profit as my long eyelashes were the bait that I would use to reel my customers in. My aunty Lily used to fall for it all the time because if she did not want any messages doing, I would start crying and the teardrops would hang on to my spider leg lashes like giant pearls. This devious plot would certainly do the trick for me and I used this routine on numerous occasions but Lily was not soft. I used to say things to her like "eh Lily, d'ya know when you were a kid" - "Did your aunties ever used to give you a Mars bar"? She would always laugh to herself and she knew the score but my cheekiness would evidently shine through to finally win her over. I would go down the stairs with my mars bar safely clutched in my grubby little hands and the wrapper would be off in two seconds flat. My hands were always minty and you could grow potatoes under my nails which is something that I never did attempt because I could not be arsed waiting for them to grow. I was referred to as Howard Hughes because I was an eccentric meff who always insisted on having my own tea cup that was indelibly marked by me. I also had my own personalised silver service that I boil washed with Daz and my pressing hygienic issues continued in the filth of my pristine existence!

My old friend and neighbour Jimmy Blakemore was a classic example of my enterprises as on most nights I would go to the chippy on Scottie Road for him. I would serve his dinner up for him in a vandalised and often pilfered tray that I had tried to disguise with the gravy. He would always order a liver dinner with no peas please at his own adamant request but if he was paying for the peas then I made damned sure that I would get them! It was quite simple and again very clever for an eight year old kid to have the audacity to ask for a liver dinner but with the peas in a separate carton. I would eat the peas before I got back to Jimmy's flat and he would always be eagerly waiting for his takeaway. He would be standing on his doorstep rubbing his hands with glee and I often felt guilty taking my reward off him. His welcoming glint of anticipation would crease me and I would still be starving but he would never offer me a chip butty for some reason. Jimmy always wore a generous smile on his face that would make me feel much better about the fact that his dinner would be minus a piece of liver and a couple of chips just for good measure. You had to be resourceful in those days and I was truly at the top of my game with no one at all to contend with!

I was always on the go and spent the long hot summer days and nights collecting all and sundry that could be utilised for me to make a decent wage. New boundaries were set and my resources would be plentiful in their apparent reward. I would add all of my new enterprises to my back catalogue of unrivalled and unsurpassed ventures and I was definitely on the road to riches. One day I would be collecting lemonade bottles for a returnable fee or cigarette coupons from the square and the next day would see me collecting rolls of copper wire. These rolls of slummy were supposedly being used as part of a massive rewiring initiative but the only thing that got a rewired was my bank account. A facelift was taking the old place back to its former glories but was it enough to spare me the pain of losing my safe house? The cigarette coupons were given to my ma and along with her Green

Shield stamps she would trade them in for the likes of a soda stream or maybe a set of pans. On one occasion she got a load of useless Tupperware which was so pointless in its crappiness that it was never ever used. We even held Tupperware parties for god sake and I am sure that the women only put up with them just to get away from their gibbering husbands. The men of the day always seemed to be drunk but they worked very hard and I suppose that they deserved a bit of pleasure. My dad was not a heavy drinker because he worked all the hours that God sent him but I guess that he made up for it on a Saturday night. We were all earning a living and I was not an exception! The copper wire was stripped of its plastic coating and then sold on to the older lads who in turn would weigh it in and we would all show a tidy profit. Everyone was part of the same trade and this chain had many links but it kept us all in a lap of relative luxury so we could not complain. This was not evident in other parts of the city centre but I suppose that everyone in the community just did what they had to do. There were many different ways to make your own few bob and I reckon that I had mastered most of them by the time I was 10 years old!

The Tory machine took hold and it threatened to strangle the very roots of a community that had strived so much to keep this city the great city that it is was. A template that was set by our ancestors was now being vandalised by a right wing government and also neglected by our left wing county council. The pigeons and sparrows had left the square and they were replaced by vultures that could be seen hovering above us in to the clear blue skies. They flew into a cloud of betrayal until it was time to attack us like something out of an Alfred Hitchcock movie. The ensuing onslaught made that Birds film look like something out of Walt Disney and they kept on coming back at us like waves of German bombers. One by one they nested in the lofts that were now depressingly vacant and they laid their eggs of doom in vast numbers. Once the greedy chicks had hatched they would grow into fledglings and they would unceremoniously kick us out of the sacred labyrinth that was once ours for keeps. Personal nest eggs were delivered to the men in the top notch Armani suits and the smart immaculate brown brogues. These men had done what even Hitler had failed to do and they did it with such ease which made it all the more sickening. Hatton Garden has a really strange twist to it and maybe it was fate that finally brought the curtains down on our own landing stage of sorts. I was all at sea but the waves of emotion were just too much for me to take on board and I searched the waters for my yellow submarine. It was never found and this octopus of a council leader used his many dodgy tentacles to spruce up his own floodlit gardens. He continued to live a life of ease within the skies of blue and the seas that were forever green with pure angst for this glorified vandal and his band of merry fossils. The men who ran us into the ground did it with no forward thinking whatsoever! They could and should have done everything in their power to keep this fabulous community alive but they split us up instead. We were all doomed but I still had a statement to make and I made the most out of what time was left for me as an under siege Gardenite!

There was life in the old dog yet and there were plenty more escapades for me to unleash on my unsuspecting crew because I now knew that I was living on borrowed time. It was a time of what seemed like a constant barrage of sunshine and with that the lure of a Lyons Maid treasure chest. I can still hear the faint echoes of a Walls ice cream van that would always be deluged by hot and bothered children and parents alike. My guilty pleasures often included the Oyster Shells or the Ninety Niner's that would be caked in syrup and topped off very nicely with a mini flake or two. Other lolly ices on offer in this mini heat wave included my favourites such as Dracula's that were sticks of black ice with a white ice cream filling and a dollop of red jelly in the middle. The bloodlike jelly just added to the drama of them living up to such a ghastly name. Also on the agenda were Frankenstein's that were green and brown and oh so very creamy in their texture.

They would just melt in your mouth to leave you feeling cool but also wanting many more of these iced delicacies. They would offer me an absorbing sensation that would last for all of 30 seconds before it evaporated and I would have to repeat this process at least five times a day. I would wait for the little yellow van to do its rounds and I followed its inviting chimes all over town. Screwballs and Twicer's were also thrown into the mix of delights that would openly display themselves on to the alluring windows of the ice cream vans. I was truly hooked on these fetishes and I would always long for the fellah with the 'lecky' ice cart to do his rounds. He would bring us all kinds of cool interlude with much needed refreshment to freeze our boiling hot tempers and to also feed our deadly addictions to sugar!

I feasted on all manner of things sweet including Beta bars or the delectable Pink Panther bars! Mmmmmmmmmmm! I can still taste them now as the munchies begin to set in and hasten to take me back to the days of Golden Cups. I loved the nutty splendour of Marathons and I still refuse to ask for their new name because I think that they have got a bloody cheek to try and change my sugar induced history. They are Marathons and will always be Marathons so why change the habit of a lifetime? I am still a rebel you see but I am forever looking for my cause because I am more of a Marlon Dingle than I will ever be a Marlon Brando but there's still time I suppose! Bring on the 'ice breaker' bars or maybe a 'finger of fudge' and maybe that would be enough for the 'Milky bars to be on me'. What I would not give now for a rhubarb and custard or even just a penny's worth of Walker's chews just to whet my appetite for a little slice of the sweet seventies extravaganza. This sugar induced decade gave many kids a set of teeth like a row of bombed houses but I managed to escape that issue. It's a good job that we got two sets of teeth really because I totally wrecked my first set of 'Dennis the Menace' gnashers but I still reckon that I need a third set! I hope that you are all munching your way through this book of goofy tales because I have never been one to mince my words. I will now move on to other former glories that will again offer you innocent captivity on a grand scale of notability!

As I continue writing this book I am daunted by the mammoth task that is required by me in order to get all of its contents just right.

The proof is in the pudding and my aim is to please everyone who will hopefully become an avid reader of my debut paperback. I don't want it to be like overkill but I do need to get in as much detail as I can to make this an enjoyable read for you all. My wish is to stoke up the fires of those who lived here with me in these happy times and to just go back to those golden days for a couple of hours or maybe even more. I hope that the people who have taken the plunge with me are now drowning in nostalgia and depending on how enlightened you are, we should all be tripping the light fantastic! I would also like for those people who are on board from an observational point of view to feel more than welcome to join in the fun. I am totally enjoying living and writing this book to the very best of my abilities as I delve further into the final throes of my anthology. Massive chances have been taken by me with this book and I have got no clue whatsoever as to how it will be received by the masses. I have a lot of faith in my crew though and it was my crew who really did prompt me to give this project a shot. Being confident is paramount to me and I know that this venture will never fall flat on its face because of its captivating honesty and its self indulgent intrigue. Call it cocky or what-evvvvvvvvvvvvver because I just see it as a gift from god that I am displaying for all of you and at last I am now the master of my destiny. I will now continue searching for my lost years and hopefully I will find them again without much further ado. Get on board my friends and follow me as I follow you on our final fling of memories made in heaven. I will add more colour to my canvas of memoirs that will be displayed in your own personal gallery of thoughts!

The one thing that I never had as a kid was a bike and I still do not know to this day why not. The reason was probably that I did not need one because the Campbell's had three and they were my mates so that's the end of that little conundrum! My best mate at the time was Michael Campbell and he taught me how to ride a bike on his purple Chopper. It even had a horn on it and had boss hand grips on the handle bars so you could do mega 'wheelies' and proper 'hand break turns'. Their Gerard had a Tomahawk and Bowler had a Budgie so you can see the pattern that was forming and my need not to own a bike. Joey Lindsay's was in a different class though because he owned a 'Commando' bike which had gears on its handle bars and was so cool in my heyday. I always remember borrowing it to go around the block and I ended up in the precinct doing wheel spins outside the Penny Farthing. Other people who I can recall with choppers in this little cycle of events were Ste Lindsay (red) and Joey O'Hara (blue) even Billy Healy had a chopper but he used that to chop our massive go kart up after bommie night. Another great mate to me over the years was Brian Duncan who was a great lad and his lovely Mother, Nellie, would always make me feel so welcome in their home. She would religiously make me tea and toast every morning when I would knock for Brian to go to school and if my memory serves me correctly then his brother Stephen was one of the first ever punk rockers to emerge from the mega glam rock era!

The punk rock scene was an affront on our bitter sweet symphonies of music that overtook the likes of Gary Glitter and Abba to be replaced by a gang of meffs in striped mohair jumpers. They used kettles for handbags and wore make up on their grids to just come across as being a little bit different. That freaked me out a bit because they were lads and I could not work out why they wanted this public image which was very limited indeed. It all added to the character of the place though and these geezers were pretty brave at the time for making such a statement that was voiced angrily by the likes of Sid Vicious or that other tit who was Johnnie Rotten. I always remember Laurence Connolly being part of the punk scene and he really was a peaceful human being but tragedy was soon to strike and it really was a shock to the system. Poor Laurence tragically passed away at a very young age and I can remember being totally gutted at the time. My last memory of him was delivering a Christmas card to our home and it was the little things like this which set him apart from other people. He had a heart of gold and his noted acts of kindness were taken on board by all who knew and loved this gentle soul. I knocked around with his brother Snowy and I can recall that the whole square was plunged into grief once again! Life is not fair I suppose and God definitely only takes the good ones first as it was proved on more than a couple of occasions. Catherine Carr was another prime example of this notion and I always remember going to see her when she was laid out to rest. She defined everything that could only be described as angelic and it was hard to believe that she was actually dead. Losing people like that at such a young age must be devastating and I would like to end this particular passage with a simple 'rest in peace' to all of those poor souls who left us way too soon!

The punk scene was an explosion of angst that was levelled at the Tory bastards in Whitehall and it even went as far as Buckingham Palace. Our dear old Queen was not immune to this tirade of youthful belligerence and her Silver Jubilee celebrations were somewhat tarnished. My teddy boy look now seemed dated and I was fuming to say the least but John Travolta burst on to the scene and once again my greased look was back in favour. The world was looking good again and I rock and rolled my way around the squares once more but not even Paul Jenkins could teach me how to dance like Danny out of Grease. The only Sandy around at this time was the legend of Holy Cross itself and that of course was Sandy Bromwell who served his community so well. He lived in Gerard Crescent before moving on to holy cross and despite his many impediments, he always stood tall as a really great ambassador of his beloved parish and beyond!

We would always seem to be playing football in the square with a Wembley trophy or a 'bladdered cazza' and if we could not get a match going then we would have a game of 'hit the post' or maybe a game of 'knockout' which would always end up in a punch up. That particular game really lived up to its name because the final result would mostly culminate in someone getting knocked out! My favourite kick about game of all time had to be 'sixty seconds' and I loved this game with an underlying passion. We delighted in the fact that we could play these games at any time at all because of the floodlights that lit up our square. If I was on my own then I would just use Tucker Peats blue transit van for target practice but his son Gerry would always leg me around the block. I would leave Gerry in my wake and I would make good my escape but at least it was something constructive to do!

Even the mums would get their kits on (thank God) and have a match amongst themselves to the delight of all the kids that would be present. They would fanatically cheer on their heroes for a share of the spoils and they were all very fervent in their allegiance. The never ending days just slumbered on into the evening chill and then on to the dusk of night time itself. The self imposed twilight would change the landscape of our castle and it was so brilliantly illuminated by our super cool floodlights. Could life get any better for me or was my time in the square slowly running out? That was a question that would always haunt me but my own sad departure was looming and I really did have to start thinking about my future! In the meantime, its back to number 7b and back to the shenanigans of my own misplaced childhood!

When my dad left the square for work in the evening we would have my mum up the wall all night and at bedtime it would always be a nightmare for her. The fun would begin in earnest as we would create havoc in the bedroom and she would come running in like Purdey off the New Avengers. She would turn all of the rings around on her fingers as if to frighten us but we were not fazed by her amateur dramatics. It just spurred us on to more evening frolics at my poor mother's expense and I went to sleep sometimes feeling really guilty. We knew that she would never hit any of us because it was never her way and we loved her for that and her other many ways of pure decency. How she held it together at times makes me now realize just how tough it must have been for her because we really did push her to the limit. I always called a halt to proceedings though because my Friday nights in front of the telly with Vincent Price were at risk and that was just too much for me to miss out on. I really did love those intimate nights with my mam and nothing was going to get in the way of my evenings spent in black and white horror. The tea and toast was just an added bonus of course and on the odd occasion I would let me ma have the elusive crust in order to keep her sweet. I could be a total pain in the arse all week but there is no way that she would ever watch Peter Cushing on her own so I really did have it made I suppose. The good times continued to roll at my own mellow pace and I lapped up every moment that was deemed to be special to me and my shadow!

Both my mum and dad worked all of the hours that God sent them and I would often tag along with me ma if only to keep me out of trouble. I liked to think that it was just her way of 'blagging' me into keeping her company on her many calls of duty. It was sometimes an ordeal for me but it offered its own rewards because I would often tempt her to visit Woolworths in town. My mouth would stream with anticipation of a two ounce bag of Raspberry Ruffles or maybe a bag of Pick and Mix. I would eat them all before we got to the till and I probably saved my poor harassed mother an absolute packet? I loved being with her and I picked up all the treats along the way but I suppose that the same could be said about most kids of this sweet laden epidemic. She shone so brightly in her own great legacy of light and I will never let this light fade away because she was a great all round character. We would go everywhere together like Hinge and Bracket and that is why I have dedicated this book to her memory and my own days spent as that sweet child of hers!

Gerard Gardens could and would go on to prove to be a very scary place to live because of the fact that it was actually built on a massive graveyard. It was evidently full of ghouls that existed in both live and dead entities but you could not really tell sometimes who was what or what was who. It was a harem full of legends and zombies alike who would be delivering all manner of ghost stories and it was definitely haunted by the lost souls of this paradise. They could find no peace in this desecrated graveyard that offered them no rest whatsoever so they walked the square in many shuddering guises. I think that everyone who had ever lived in this spooky place would each have their own terrifying stories to tell in their own indelible way but for now at least, here are a few of my own!

My uncle Willie Shields who was married to my aunty Hannah (my biggest fan) would often come to our house after closing time in the pub and he would make himself comfortable on our Lorraine's Bontempi keyboard. This stylish organ had all of the haunting notes built in and so the scene was gruesomely set for an hour long slice of drunken inebriated terror! We would be mesmerised and hung on to his every chilling word because he was a great ghost story teller. He delivered all of the glory and gory bits with a fine panache whilst hitting the keyboard with all the drama of 'Tales of the Unexpected'.

All of his stories flowed and just added to the intrigue of our square and beyond the four walls that protected us so vehemently. As much as we were scared out of our Mister Men pyjamas, we absolutely loved the fear that he would generate and we would always want more from him because he delivered his stories with so much conviction. This came about routinely as he would miss the last bus home to Kirkby and he would happily crash down on our couch. He would feed us on pure nerves and we would scream out loud at some of his terrifying instalments. I reckon that he only stayed in our house because he had actually ended up scaring himself into a blind panic and there is no way that he would ever attempt to get home on his own. He would not walk the square alone for fear of being attacked by the bogeyman and we loved the fact that he had probably put the jitters up himself. The night always mellowed out with him playing his mouth organ to the tune of 'Walk on' or maybe even the more pleasing and appropriate 'Z' cars theme if we were lucky. Willie the conqueror would never admit to the latter because he was a staunch red nose and he would never have lived it down if our Jim or our Stephen had ever found out. Well, your secret is out now Willie, and I am going to tell everyone at your Joe's 'next' wedding. My nana Parry always had a good tale to tell too as did most of my family which was befit of many story tellers and amazing people who I was totally blessed to be a part of. They are all legends and they are all people that I love and thank wholeheartedly for everything that they ever involved me in. They displayed their worth so lovingly at the various stages of my own tales from the crypt and it has always been noted by me!

Legends like 'Kick the Can' or 'Spring Heeled Jack' stick out in my mind profusely because as far as I can gather, they were ghosts of the friendly kind. In the dead of night you would be awoken to the sound of a can being kicked around the square but you would never see the person who was actually kicking it or even the can itself! To me it was not scary at all and in a way it was quite comforting to know that such ghosts would still frequent our square. There were ghosts and fables everywhere and even our house was haunted in a big way as we were soon to find out with a cold shudder. I am not kidding you and I will tell you these stories in exactly the same way that I have told you all of my other stories. Please beware and just for safety, grab yourself a hammer and a torch just in case. My tales of terror may appear farfetched about these not so living souls but they really did exist in these times of 'Shiver and Shake'. They are being played out through the eyes of a smitten child who is just relaying his own surreal and dramatic accounts in order to give you a real taste of these scary times. I witnessed strange goings on in our house from a very early age and my family can vouch for me as to what I am about to tell you. We even had a resident 'Peeping Tom' in our midst and he terrorised the squares for ages. He was finally apprehended one night and systematically beaten up for his sordid peeping ways. When the beating was done they left him out to dry and the 'scrawny' pied wagtails feasted on him. I hope that these minty pigeons pecked the bleeder's eyes out so that he could never repeat his crimes ever again!

This leads me on to the times when we would go looking for 'Mick's' in St. John's Gardens with a big bag of corn and a noose that was made out of either cotton or twine. We would catch the birds and take the rings off their feet and then trade in the different coloured rings to the highest bidder. He would be the keenest collector of these multi-coloured bands and I never really saw the point in this cruel sport. After hours of toiling in the hot sun and bird shit, we would return home to the square and we would go home to watch the latest episode of the 'Professionals' or maybe catch the end of 'Starsky and Hutch'. We were like homing pigeons and we would settle down for the night after a long day out in the realms of our very own playground. I found a 'youngie' one day and it could not fly so I brought it home with me to see if my wildlife skills could be pushed to their limits. We nursed this fluffy chick back to health with bread and water and then stood on the veranda to watch it take off on its maiden voyage. It flew straight into a bus on Christian Street and that was the end of this poor bird's very swift albeit deadly existence. It went from the relative safety of an eggshell to a dramatic and sad conclusion in a nut shell.

St. John's Gardens was a happy hunting ground for me because it was also the place where I would uproot my ma's daffodils. It was also the place that gave me hours and hours of unadulterated adventure with my own breed of decent looking birds. I would proceed to dig out these daffodils with all the precision and skill of that Texas chain saw massacre fellah as I plucked away menacingly at this flowery sea of yellow. She got them every year on Mother's Day with the all roots still attached for authenticity and the smile on her face would somehow exonerate my mini crime spree. I was well and truly off the hook but I would need some more daffodils so I would head off back to St. John's Gardens. I would get a job lot and give them to my two nanas on the landing and all of my aunties who would be present in the commune at this very motherly time. It would be my way of just saying thank you to all of them and also a sure fire way to receive some expenses for my hard days graft in the muck. I continued with my own version of bird watching in and around town but I still could not find that elusive girl who would finally tie me up or down. I was not all that fussy really but I guess that the girl of my dreams was, and I spent endless days just waiting for my chance to pounce. I am 43 years old now and along with everything else, my dreams have shrivelled up but there is always hope I suppose. I will be hunting once again at my book launch that has now been finalised and it will happen at the Liner Hotel in Lord Nelson Street on November 19th 2010. Everyone is invited to what will be the most defining moment of my life and my nerves have gone at the very prospect of me putting my name up in lights. It has been a long time coming and I am buzzing to feck now because my mother will be so proud of me!

The whole area around the museum was great for me because it incorporated so many great buildings and of course we had our very own fountain that was used by me on many occasions. It would always be when I came out of 'John's Gardens' covered in mud following my daffodil exploits and in me needing a good scrub before I ventured home. The fountain was always dead handy for me because it was just a very ornate bathroom that also doubled up as a massive commode. I reckon that many kids used this fountain as a piss pot but I never ever did a number two in there and that's the Gods honest truth! It also gave grace to the famous 'giant's grave' and of course the 'giant steps' that were really hard to climb due to this relics enormity. We even had our own 'little Wembley' where we could only play 'five a side' football because the pitch was so small but the turf was like a lush green carpet. Being a bit of a scammer would also entail that my best mate was a little Asian lad whose name escapes me for now but his free ice creams certainly did not. His dad owned the ice cream van that was parked outside these gracious buildings and again my resourcefulness shone brighter than the setting sun that would descend rather fittingly behind the Walker Art Gallery. This gallery served me well because it was my enlarged page three of *The Sun* newspaper and I would study all the pictures in great detail to see what beards were real and what beards were in fact otherwise. I spent hours studying the otherwise and compared them to the scores of other fit nudies that were displayed on the walls and ceilings of the fabulous Philharmonic Hall. It had always struck me as being odd as to why these portraits of beauty appeared to be so well hung when my own crown jewels were barely distinguishable. I envied these painted artefacts and I hoped that one day I would be able to match their modesty but unfortunately, I am still waiting. All the lead weights in the world could not help my inferior predicament and I have given up the fight for now but science is a wonderful thing!

The museum was a very interesting place but only if you did not go inside because it used to just bore the arse off me. I only ever enjoyed going in there to try and get my hands on the treasure trove of coins that were calling me from the wishing well by the entrance. I remember the light blue Ford Anglia and that little cobbled Victorian Street but apart from that and maybe those mummified geezers, I would give this antiquated place a wide berth. I happily continued my adventures outside because that is where it was all happening and I was always up for some action. One such time was when the old Stork Hotel in Queens Square was in a bad state of disrepair. The 'box of toys' would use this old ruin to hone our skills as rock climbers and we reached many summits in our quest to be the most daring. It was a very dangerous building but that just added to the excitement of it all and I am still here today to tell you my story from the dizzy heights of my plateau. There were masses of dilapidated warehouses and buildings in our midst and these dwellings offered us lots of adventure at the very minimal fee of just cuts and bruises. I loved getting into scrapes and I would come home sometimes like a casualty of war but my mother would always be waiting in the barracks and she always nursed me back to health! She was awarded the purple heart for her actions with the words "I love you" written on the front of these little medals of honour. They were in fact tubes of multi coloured sweets that were called "Love hearts" and I used these little tokens for all kinds of missions!

The subways by Transport House even offered us plenty of solace and we would use the sloping walkways as a massive skateboard run. The kids of the day would turn into 'Evel Knievel' as they practised and completed many cupid stunts that would put the kids of today to shame. This army of dare devils mastered the art of jumping over six milk crates and landing in a crumpled heap at the bottom of the subway. We were all completely bonkers and we would defy the laws of gravity but it was these laws that kept us out of serious trouble. It was full of danger but this just added to the mayhem of this vast playground that was uniquely ours and boy did we utilise everything that we had in our grasp. The concreted hills at the side of the stairs would double up as our ski slopes and we would use the old orange traffic cones as our improvised sleds. On one occasion, I completely ripped the skin off my arse as we held our own unique version of the winter Olympics. I fell off my cone but carried on down the slope like 'Eddie the Eagle' and ended up having to go to hospital again. The subway was also our safe passage from the ever growing traffic system that was a blot on our landscape and contributed to what was to become our impending downfall! The old place was going down the drain and instead of trying to put things right everybody had basically just given up!

My days of detonators and match bombs were drawing to a close but I was oblivious to it all because I just blanked it all out. I made the most out of my ever impending days in this coliseum that was well and truly my established homeland. I was dreading the very thought of leaving it all behind me but there was nothing at all that I could do to save these Victorian catacombs. The vultures were now homing in on us and my mum and dad were well aware of this fact but they 'brassed' it out for as long as they possibly could. They tried to keep it from us because they knew that we would be totally gutted to be finally leaving our coveted place of birth. I was in self-denial but I kept my beady eyes firmly fixed on the looming disaster and just prayed to God that it was just another nightmare. It was not to be and I completely lost my faith and almost lost the will to live because my happiness was just being ripped away from me. Was God losing his fight with that firebrand fellah downstairs and was my divine sanctuary going to give way to the horrors of an impending Devil's playground? I will now go from one horror story to another and on to a tale that I never got around to earlier on in this mini biography. Please accept my apologies for wittering on and I am sorry if I keep losing the plot in this book but certain things just keep popping up into my mind and I just want to try and get them all in!

This unexpected tale is about the strange goings on that occurred to me one night as I was searching for Christmas presents. It was on a particular night when I thought that curiosity would definitely kill the cat or at least as in my case, kill this kitten! One night when my mum and dad were out socialising, I was rooting in their room as I often did around Christmas time and I was looking behind their wardrobe. It was very dark as I recall with just the glow of the yellow street lamps illuminating the pitch black room. Suddenly and very clearly I heard the voice of an old man call out my mother's name and I literally froze on the spot. "Pat" he called out, in a low and gravelly voice which prompted me to scream out loud and quickly call off my search for my goodies. I ran to the safety of my bedroom but I was scared shitless and my need for sanctuary overwhelmed me. I was screaming hysterically at our Franky and Lorraine because of what I had just heard behind the wardrobe and they too were spooked out of their skins. They joined me on the landing and we ran along to Katie Daltons and hammered on her door like a pack screaming banshees. The hysterics on show must have frightened poor Katie too because it was pretty late and 'Kick the can' was doing his rounds. Katie was our next door neighbour and someone who we doted on along with her loving husband Davey. Between them they were always on call for us no matter what and we had them up the wall sometimes with our innocent but time consuming exploits. They were there at a moment's notice in our many hours of need and nothing was ever too much trouble for them. Katie came back in with us and she sat us down as she proceeded with her own ghostly investigations. Her and Davey comforted us until my mum and dad came back home at around midnight unaware of my call from beyond the grave. After telling them about my brief encounter with a ghost my mother glanced at my dad and they reassured me that it was just my over active imagination. They left me to just get on with it but I knew what I had heard that night and it was only years later that I found out the reassuring but ghostly truth!

My grandfather Shields who I never knew and my nana had lived in number 7b before my mum and dad had moved in and unfortunately my 'old pops' had died before I had the pleasure of ever meeting him. It transpired that the mystery man who I had encountered all those years ago was in fact him and he just wanted to say hello. This clarified a lot of other strange goings on at the time and we would all encounter them but we also dismissed them as a fact that our house was just spooky. On a number of occasions I would hear footsteps in the hall and faint breathing which was heavy but not threatening in any way at all. The footsteps would coincide with the sound of the toilet light getting switched on followed by a pause and then the sound of the light being switched back off again. The footsteps would then disappear and all would be quiet again but it happened on a number of occasions and mostly when my mum and dad were out. We just got used to it because it was a presence that was both comforting and reassuring to me but not to our kid as he was about to find out for himself. I would actually look forward to hearing this routine being played out over and over again but still I would pull the covers over my head just in case. I was sad not to have met Joseph (in human form) or my uncle Jim who died very young and also my other uncle Tony who himself departed at a very young age. They all left a massive hole in all of our lives but we were compensated by everyone who had surrounded us with care and a love that was always received with gratitude. As we get older we inevitably lose loved ones but all of my great family who have since left us will always remain very much a part of us. God bless you all and rest in peace! I will now continue my story of our kid's own night of horror and one that put him off Doctor Who for life!

The scariest thing that ever happened in our house of horrors was to happen to our Franky and it really did put the shits up the lot of us including my mum and dad who themselves witnessed this spooky and terrifying apparition. This spooky hollow was to present itself to our kid and any doubts that he may have harboured about my own fables were smashed to smithereens. He woke up screaming one night and was in utter turmoil because of what he had just seen coming from the ceiling light. He was woken up by the spooky presence of whom or whatever it was and the figure stood over him as he screamed out loud. It was noted that this ghost had a friendly agenda but our kid was not aware of this fact and he tried to exorcise this demon with his tears. He described the ghostly figure as looking like 'Doctor Who' with his grey wispy hair and a man whose features appeared to be that of an old timer. This spiritual being never harmed our kid but he touched his face and attempted to tuck him into bed but Franky was having none of it. The figure disappeared when he became inconsolable and again it was put down to too much television and a very vivid imagination. He knew that what he had seen and heard that night was not a dream because it was so real and things started adding up. What he had experienced under the cover of darkness would stay with him forever and Scoobydoo was banned in our flat for the foreseeable future. After this incident our kid moved into my bedroom and he went to bed every night with a 'sky beamer' by his side and a bottle of that 'Hail Mary water' just in case.

When we weren't chasing ghosts away, we would use the torch to make our very own 'Odeon' cinema but the films were not very good at all. The only Oscar winning performance would go to my ma when she would run in to do her 'Purdy' routine. It was not all that often though because we were good kids really and the family drama was limited to the silver screen. I remember a lad called Paul Sudbury who was a bit of film buff himself and he made all of his own films in and around Gerard Gardens. He would charge 'two bob' for us to get into his 'kung fu' flicks and they were actually very good under the limited circumstances. Paul went on to do a film which actually featured me and it is called "Gardens of stone". It is a brilliant collaboration and I was very proud to be asked for my contribution on this piece of Gerard Gardens history. He also wrote a book of the same name and I feature in this book quite often which is a real privilege for me. Gerard Fagan also wrote a book about our famous tenements called *In a City Living* but I am still waiting for my signed copy off him! I wish that I could stop jangling and just get on with my own frigging book now because I am giving myself a massive headache and I need to continue with my own horror sequel!

We often speak about these ghostly times and it was only later on in life that we learned that it was in fact my grandfather who was making these ghostly apparitions. He was basically just looking over us from the realms of his own world and I was very sad not to have ever met him in person. This world is now looked back upon in fondness and it just added to the greatness of our home and our happy if not scary childhood memories. To see us through these scary nights, my mum and dad used to leave the radio on in the kitchen to ward off any strange noises that would frighten us. The calming air waves would give us a restful night of sleep and our dreams would be fully restored in our very own land of nod. These Scoobydoo escapades were oh so real to me and this pesky kid was always meddling about in someone else's not so spirited business! Being built on a massive graveyard gave way to some other eerie goings on and whenever ground work was being carried out in the area, the skeletons would appear in numbers. They were definitely not of the cupboard kind and this particular 'big dig' unearthed many bags of bones. I remember work being done in St. John's Gardens and there were skulls and various other bones everywhere but this did not faze me at all. I had witnessed all of these gruesome scenes before on the silver screen so it was nothing new to me. Unfortunately for the skulls, their only purpose now was to be used as footballs but I never did see anyone scoring a diving header with one of these skeletal 'casey's'. I did however witness loads of them being dumped unceremoniously in the famous fountain on William Brown Street and the 'steble' fountain resembled a giant bowl of 'scouse'. The spooky games of football would invariably end up in deadlock with a bone of contention that would be only resolved by way of a penalty shootout. If that did not produce a winner then the game would go to sudden death and proceedings would draw to a happy if not scary conclusion. No wonder we got haunted you might say but we did not care because it was part of our uniqueness that we prided ourselves on. The shallow graves were just another part of this adventure playground that was teeming with ghouls or maybe goals would be a more fitting anecdote to such unearthly goings on!

To forgive our sins we would have to go to church every Sunday and you could not miss church for any reason whatsoever because it was just the right thing to do in these most divided of days. The division being the Catholic and Protestant religion with the latter being carried out in the name of that silly 'King Billy fellah'! Every Sunday morning we would be praying and playing with our pipes of peace but our peace would often be broken by these little bleeders. A gang of dudes with ginger hair and limps would break up our holy matrimony by banging a big drum outside our church. This posse would leave the parishioners absolutely fuming to say the least and it caused all kinds of trouble on the streets because we were being purposely provoked. This 'lazzie' band of not so merry men were better known as the 'Orange Lodge' and they marched onto the boundaries of our own loyal Catholic faith. They would walk down from Netherfield Road and do our heads in on purpose but we would always be waiting for them with our artillery of bricks. It was a hard faced affront which led to many pitched battles over the years and some of the fighting was pretty violent at the time. It is very funny how the initials of this 'out of order' gang would spell 'LOL' which in today's terms evidently means "Laugh out loud"! These urchins were not welcome to walk in our parish and we let them know in no uncertain terms of endearment!

The outdated vegans would throw pepper into our eyes and they marched on to their own misguided days of glory in a haze of alcohol. They would noisily march to Southport for nothing more than a gargle and a scrap with some local gypsies and they would come home in a right state. We would take revenge on these 'Scotchies' by randomly bricking them as they made their way home from their annual day out by the seaside. The ugly scenes would be acted out in a blaze of piss and orange frizzy hair that was always dead easy to 'wool' all over the place. We would relentlessly attack these gimps from the safe confines of the subways that were a perfect rat run for us to make good our escape. There would be bloody mayhem as we fought our consecrated battles out of loyalty to our Papal pride which we held so close to our green and white emblazoned hearts. We would send these orange 'out of order' men packing but the hostilities just escalated and the area around Everton Road became a definite no go area. Our obvious dismay was voiced angrily and violently as we would in turn really make them pay for imposing on us by wrecking their parades. A riot of magnitude and mayhem would ensue and again there would be fists and tufts of ginger hair flying everywhere.

I guess that the open warfare displayed from both sides was just a sign of the times really and all is forgiven now as we moved on in a peaceful if not divided state of harmony. Everyone was really religious in those troubled times and we all loved our faith because it had served us so well in times of despair and our faith also instilled the beliefs that would deliver us from evil.

The troubles left me questioning what it was all about in my own kingdom of God and theirs but thankfully our faiths have now embraced each other. I have many good friends and family in the Orange Order and today's troubles only consist of banter thank God. The perfect solution would be to just unite these two great faiths into one unique army of Christians and together we could take on all of the infidels who choose to wreak havoc on our shores. It is great that we have settled our differences now because our great country must be made aware of the Muslim uprising that threatens us every single day. I like the Muslim faith but I do not want to see us as a Muslim state because we would inherit their somewhat draconian ways. I would much rather be one of Hitler's babies than be one of these silly mad mullah freaks but I must add that this is only a minority. The Muslim faith in general is great but there are some evil bastards out there who are deranged with their sick and over the top beliefs. All practising faiths should be duly respected and tolerance should be taught at every level in order for us to coexist. We do not kill in the name of God and that should be respected by the few who wish our soldiers dead in Afghanistan. These cheeky bums of terror take the piss out of us whilst they are milking our country for freebies and they are funding a war that is directed at the very hand that feeds them. Every single decent faith including the Muslim faith should stand together and rid the world of these despicable men in order to proclaim the benefits of world peace! My own faith in the church is solid and I inherited my many obligated beliefs from what I was being taught in my own 'ministry of sound' that was being played out to me every Sunday!

Father Baker would deliver his own sermon as usual with all the damnation that you would come to expect from a man of the cloth. He was a very imposing man and he sometimes struck fear into me with his deliverance of the many gospels that he would spout out from his pulpit. God was the almighty but I did not agree with his way of spreading the word because it just instilled fear into kids and that just did not seem right. He would contrive to scare the sinners of the parish to change their wicked lives and their very existence of debauchery and drink but I was not convinced. If they did not agree to mend their ways then they would burn in hell forever with Satan and his mates and that was really scary to me. I instilled my own set of beliefs from within and I served the church from a different point of view but I always considered myself a firm believer. I loved God and the whole bible thing but I always preferred the Dave Allen version which was being played out on the BBC in front of millions of viewers. My mother hated him with a vengeance but he was just putting his own views across about what was wrong with our faith and I thought that he was spot on. He was far more convincing than any of our own priest's biblical and disproportionate psalms on what I could and could not do and I gracefully took his views on board.

Kids should not be subjected to parade as angels out of fear of being demonised for simply being a little bit wayward and I was no exception. We were taught that if you were naughty then you would be sent to hell for all eternity and I am not overly exaggerating this fact. This notion was being force fed to me by these bible bashing men on an everyday basis and I really do prefer the approach that the modern church has now undertaken. Dave Allen's light hearted views about our faith sometimes took away from the scary scriptures that were levelled at me on a Sunday because I did not really care about being a 'goody two shoes'. It is not right to fear a priest and I really did as a kid but I made up for it by just believing in Father Christmas because he definitely got it right all the time. This saint would give us presents even if we had been naughty and his own jolly sermons were given and received with lots of ho, ho, ho! I did not like church but would go along and just take it all in and then I would just go back to my own self proclaimed life because after all I was just a kid. Another father who I warmed to was Father Abraham whose flock consisted of little blue 'Smurfs' who lived in 'Smurf land'. I loved his teachings and his little blue congregation of 'Smurfs' would blissfully spread the word of this great man to all who would listen!

My faith today is very strong because I understand the teachings now but there is no way that I would force them on to my children because in my eyes, it is not God's way. Children should be allowed to make choices for themselves in order for our faith to survive because there is a lot of apathy about at the moment and we are slowly losing our status. We should rebuild our churches instead of pulling them down and there should be a massive drive for Christians to stand together in the face of adversity. This would be a way to retain our identity in a country that has gone to the dogs and nobody is doing anything at all to rectify this problem of biblical proportions. Instead of hanging on to the altar rails for salvation, people should practice their faith by being decent human beings and the world would be a much better place to pray in. My rant is over and I actually feel like Father Baker now but my sermon is one of love for the church that my mother served so religiously like the good Catholic woman that she was!

Apart from church on a Sunday it would be a great day for us because we all sat down to a Sunday roast dinner and enjoyed watching match of the day on our black and white television. You could never tell who it was playing but we watched it anyway because it was enthralling and we did not have much televised football in those days. We would marvel at the skills of the great football teams and the exceptional individuals on show but it was all so very confusing to me. The commentator would try to help us figure out who it was in possession of the ball and it would only be made easier if Newcastle united were playing? The BBC brought the beautiful game into the comforts of our home and as spectators we would be glued to our seats for an hour of pure footy indulgence. After watching the football we would delve into the delights of me ma's homemade cooking and she really did excel in the art of making an apple pie. She would spend all day cooking and cleaning our small flat with Abba or the Carpenters on full blast, until of course the football came on the telly. My poor ma played second fiddle to our fanatical ways but she always played a blinder as the perfect host to our varied needs. I never went to watch Everton in those days for some unknown reason and it was that unknown reason that made me change my allegiance for a few weeks. My aunty Joan Allen was a red nose and she offered to take me to Anfield so I thought "why not"? I never really settled as a reds fan but at least I was going to the match and Joan always bought me a Mars bar and a cup of tea at half time so thanks Joan!

It was a period of greatness for Liverpool FC who reigned supreme at the time and they won everything that was put before them. They did it with a swagger of seemingly great ease and just brushed aside the other great teams of this depressing era. They were brilliant and were led by the late and great Bill Shankly who guided them on to many honours and who broke the hearts of the many Evertonians on show including myself. We could only watch in awe as they went on to achieve everything that was possible in football and it was a time that still haunts me forever because I was forced to be a red. It was a nightmare going into school on a Monday because I would be teased all morning about the fact that we were born losers. It weighed very heavily on my mind and to alleviate my pain I just jumped ship and on to the glory trail that was painted red and white. I had interbred with the devil himself to bare my soul as a bloody red nose and my dad was gunning for me. It was deemed to be a cardinal sin at the time and totally unheard of because if you were born a blue it was seen as a blessing. I had sinned and I had to pay the ultimate price to become a blue again by throwing away the red shackles that had nearly changed my faith. I was made to repent in front of a legend that was to present itself to me as William Ralph Dean. I had heard about this great man many times and as he looked down on me from my bedroom wall, I realized that I had made a dreadful mistake. I was torn in two and it would take some divine intervention by my dad to finally convince me to see the error of my ways!

I had been revelling in my new found guise as a follower of the 'shite' and I basked in their glory but my dad had other plans for me. The order was made for me to change my allegiance back to his beloved Everton but I was having none of it. We were embarking on a holiday to sunny Torquay at the time and the day before we were due to leave my dad laid his cards on the glass coffee table. He informed me that I would not be going on holiday unless I became a blue again and I was in bits. After much deliberation I agreed to his request and so my love affair with Everton was re-acquainted and everyone was now happy in their blue heaven including me. Going to watch the blues did not materialise despite my 'U' turn and I had to make do with a radio and maybe 5 minutes on a Sunday afternoon. We still never won anything but I loved them anyway and for that I thank my dad for making me see the light and getting my own taste of glory in the 1980s. It was a long time to wait but oh so worth it for the times that I would experience as a liberated 'blue boy'. I put my transgression of being a red down to the fact that I liked Dave Allen and God was just getting me back for my sins. It miraculously worked and I go to church every week now in an Everton kit and yes there is definitely a blue heaven way beyond my blue moon.

Every time Liverpool won something and it would seem like every week they would hold a massive parade in the centre of town. There would be thousands of fans from all over the country and a few hundred from the city itself to lead and cheer their heroes on. It was an amazing sight but one that depressed the blue half of the city as we could only watch in despair. We inadvertently joined in the spectacle that would become so common practice for the reds because it was all around the city centre. People from Iraq and Poland would join forces with the thousands of other fans from Norway and Sweden to savour what must have seemed like a massive home game for the reds supporters. The four corners of the square would be a mass of red and white flags with an abundance of bunting that was only ever surpassed by the Queens Silver Jubilee in 1977. I always remember Joey O 'Hara having a big red and white Canadian flag and it really did stick out amongst the other many flags that were out on display in these very depressing times.

As much as I hated these times of glory, it still gives me happy memories and a glow inside if only to say that I had actually witnessed the furore! When Bill Shankly announced that he was leaving the glare and imposing stench of the famous 'Spion Kop' there was a sense of relief from the massed ranks of the blue half. We had suffered this man for so long and we were just glad to just see the back of him. We mocked our counterparts on their demise but it was very short lived as Bob Paisley took over the reigns and the supposed poison chalice that was meant to herald the end of Liverpool's overpowering dominance. We even coined a song about their fall from grace with the tune being from Showaddywaddy's iconic song "hey rock and roll'. It went something like this... ("Hey rock and roll---- Shankly's on the dole---- don't forget to mention---- Paisley's on a pension") Unfortunately for us bluenoses it was short lived and a new era would begin where the former had left off. It was a reign that saw Liverpool enjoy unrivalled success for another lengthy period of time and the not so mighty blues languished in the doldrums of mediocrity for a number of soul destroying seasons. We had our moments but I am afraid to say that none of them were ever really that great but all the same I was proud to be a blue boy and I just got on with it. We had Bob Latchford and Duncan McKenzie amongst others and they gave us many magical moments with 'moments' being the key word. I will quickly move on now to a time when football took a back seat for me and to a time when I was inadvertently summonsed by God to serve him at the altar of all things decent and velvet!

Every aspect of this place was a celebration for me and when I made my first holy communion it was a really big event for all the kids or should I say, all of the mums. They were trying their very best to outdo each other and we were the unassuming pawns in this battle of the frills. It was a competition of pride and joy that would sweep the whole parish and the daggers were definitely being drawn from all quarters. A celebration of faith transformed itself into one of bias as to how the kids would turn out on this holiest of days and my family were no exception. There has been an open debate over the years as to who actually made my suit and one that I have never got to the bottom of. My aunty Lily and my cousin Marie Murphy have both laid claim as to whoever made me inherit my 'Bobby crush' look but I think that they were both instrumental in my cuteness. I find the pair of them guilty to the charge of treason and for giving me more frills than a new born baby girl. The suit that they made for me was an absolute whopper and I reckon that their joint effort easily won me the title of the best dressed kid on communion Sunday. I had found God but would he find me or find out about my many misdemeanours before confession?

Getting back to my communion day and the really proud day it was for me and especially my mum. She spent an absolute fortune on my velvet suit with all the trimmings and all the finishing touches that would be required to make me look the part on my special day. Extras like my 'no frills' frills and my white Gatsby shoes were thrown into the mix to make me look and feel like a Burtons dummy. I was pristine and looked like an angel as did all of the other kids but I definitely reckon that I stole the show or at least that was what I was led to believe. We all went to church and posed for the obligatory photo shoot and then made our way around every corner of the squares to get our reward for being and looking so holy. The whole angelic scene was always captured through the lens of a very seasoned and brilliant photographer of his day called, Georgie 'Bonus'. We called him that name because he would always give you a framed bonus print if you paid up early and on the dotted line for his mesmerising stills. Naaaaaaaa! I am only kidding because George Bowness was in fact his real name and he produced nearly every photograph in and about the squares at the time. He would take us little mop top urchins and he would transform us into the smiling princes and princesses of a lost crusade that we would all aspire to. It did not last for long though as I returned to my 'Damien' mode and back to the square for more of my innocent wrongdoings. I could get away with anything now because I was holy and any minor indiscretions would be wiped out by some act of contrition. For somebody in my white shoes this was great and my sacred beliefs were firmly bequeathed on me in the form of redemption. I wore my black velvet kecks right up to the much celebrated evening when I was sitting on a radiator in my mother's work and I slipped accidently on purpose. I unceremoniously ripped them to shreds and finally I got rid of these Gregorian pantaloons forever. My shoes got dyed black and I wore them for school until they went grey and fell off my feet while I was playing 'togger' in the school yard. Oh happy days indeed!

Lily the pink is my wonderful godmother and my ma's sister who is happily married to my uncle Danny O 'Connell who himself is a top geezer and a real fighter for his cause. They lived above my nana on the 'holy block' in the crescent with their two kids and my cousin's Danny and Kevin. I think it was little Danny who got me into Showaddywaddy because he was very much into the 'teddy boy' scene. He could never match my famous dance moves though even though he was a regular mover and shaker on the disco scene of this 1970s dancing inferno. I liked his taste of music but I really did draw the line at his Doctor Hook tendencies and other bands like Wishbone Ash!

This celebrated era of 'illuminated' pink socks and crepe soles was a blast for everyone who proudly donned the full regalia of a true rock 'n' roller. Kevin could dance but it would only be on a football pitch because I always remember him being a really good player. He would often grace the hallowed tarmac of the Crescent like the Bobby dazzler that he was and he went on to be a real life dazzling Bobby on the beat. Lily and her crew suffered my nonchalance but they also loved me and I loved every single one of them back with all of my heart. They would not change anything at all about their time here as they were also very proud to have been happy dwellers of this great place. I had them all harassed really but I reckon that they just enjoyed it like I always did but sometimes they did not show it. Even if I did get a kick up the arse of my 'kecks' from time to time I did not mind at all because I had always warranted it. I would always run away laughing and skitting at them as they angrily "effed and blinded" at me from the landing down to the old stairway to heaven. The very next day would always see me back for another instalment of 'Bless this house' because after all, this was the "Holy Block"!

My nana lived with my uncle Mike who was a belter and he was dead funny but I always had them tormented with by 'asbo' antics. I learned most of my 'comic caper' ways off our Mike because he would just blow me away with his humour and I thank him for being my master of comedy. He definitely got taught by my nana though who was the undoubted Queen of giggles because she was so very captivating. My poor nana and our Mike were hounded by me but they put up with it because I was a loveable rogue and they were just as bad as me. Mike was in a band at the time called 'Lilac wine' and they went on a mammoth world tour of hundreds of social clubs that were dotted about these rock star confines. He even threw a telly out of a hotel window once but it did not count as notoriety because it was a black and white portable. He will kill me now for being economical with the truth but I am only having a laugh 'Bert' and it was you who taught me how to be funny so chill out! Auntie Cissie was my nana's sister and she had a daughter called Marie who now lives next door but one to Lily on Everton Road. They were very posh and affluent in their demure way but they were both very gracious women. You could always tell when a visit was imminent because the telly would get turned off at their insistence and the posh talk would ensue. They fascinated me with their tales of a bygone era but I would be left fuming because I would be missing Hickory House or Pipkins on the telly. It was cool though and I always looked forward to greeting these two fine women because they were an establishment in their own right!

I was luckily surrounded by lovely people who intermingled with each other and who all contributed massively to my sound upbringing. It is a massive family that I feel very proud to be a part of and we retain that notion on our many social gatherings. I cannot wait for my book launch because it is a sort of thank you to all of my family and friends who have been there for me. Especially to my immediate family who have all had a really tough time lately with the sad passing of my mother and other heartbreaking news from within our tight knit union. I hope we are turning the corner now because we have been battered from pillar to post with bad news but there are real signs of a positive future. The worst thing about having such a big family is the fact that they ultimately pop their clogs and it really does seem unfair with every sad passing. I will never get over my mother's untimely departure but bringing my family together will bring me and them some kind of welcome comfort. I do not know how many white feathers I am going to find and collect on my travels because I have found literally tonnes of them. I am in the process of actually making my own eiderdown with them and at this rate I will have the matching pillows in no time at all. My mother is forever in my thoughts and she has been with me throughout this book in every single word that I have written. Her presence will be felt by all on my big night and I will celebrate her legacy in the best way possible that is befitting of this beautiful woman. I did it ma and I am 'top of the world' happy to be finally shouting it from the rooftops. This great place was teeming with great people who all shared in the grand mêlée of these art deco inhibitions and I will now return to those special 'lava lamp' days of oblivion!

On one occasion our Mike asked me to go to the mobile van for him and asked me to get him ten No6 as he often did. He said "If they have not got any No6 lad then get me anything", so I just got him a Mars bar instead because to me "anything" meant "any thing" so I guess that I got it right the first time! Mike took us out a few times with my aunty Sue and our baby 'Lou Lou' who will now be made up that I have mentioned her in this book because she badly wants to 'geg' in on the Gardens crew. We went to Chester Zoo on one occasion and we had a really good time even though we never actually got in. It was a laugh anyway and my fingers are still hurting from the antics of some of them really cheeky monkeys! These great times will always be remembered and it is my job to make these memories remain in indelible ink!

I visited all of my aunties and uncles on a regular basis because each household would offer me something completely different.

Playing swing ball with my cousins in Everton Brow or having water fights in Cantril Farm would always be appealing but I always loved coming back to my spiritual home. As much as I loved my jaunts to the countryside, it would always be nice to just spend some time in my own confines with my brother and my sister. They were a massive part of my childhood but they themselves had loads of friends so our paths only really crossed in our home. We spent lots of cherished times together and they were forever on the periphery of my wrong doings but they would join in the fun with their own little misdemeanours. We all have our own enchanting memories of childhood and my wish is to just whet your appetite a little and to reawaken your own great times spent in the squares. Everyone else who is reading this book will agree with me that we were living in a time capsule that would remain dormant forever unless it was invigorated. I will keep these fabulous memories alive by giving you my best shot and I will now turn on the style in every sense of the word!

Style was very apparent in the 1970s and Adi Dassler was at the height of the fashion chain along with one Frederick Perry. They were both revered as being mightily cool and a must for every kid in the square to be seen in because they were the true masters of style. I had a pair of Adidas 'blackbird' that were black and yellow and the same colours as my Fred Perry tee shirt so my look was complete. These fashion passions gave me prominence in the glare of the square and this made me feel so cool amongst my fellow advocates. It was not always that way though and I must admit that I hated my 'two tone' stacks and my sick 'Birmingham bags' that would go on to haunt me forever. I got them for Easter and when I went to church you could hear the 'clip, clop, clip' of my platform shoes. They were that high that I got vertigo and I nearly fell over my high heels in the church aisle. I steadied myself and continued forward much to the amusement of Tommy O 'Keefe. Tommy was another legend of our time and he deserves a big mention in this book for his services to St. Joseph's church and parish. The pockets in my 'high waist' bags were massive and you could easily fit three Easter eggs into each one if you took the packaging off them. There would even be enough room for a couple of crème eggs and maybe two packets of Maltesers.

Fashion was a big thing in the 70s and we all had our own little disasters but none more so than me with my German 'lederhosen' leather pants. They were disgusting and I hated them because I looked like something out of 'Swiss Miss' and Oliver Hardy had nothing on me. The only 'lonesome pine' that I could see was me and I would cry myself to sleep at the very thought of these bondage gear efforts. I don't know where me ma got these from but they would not have been out of place in a frigging war museum or in any 'Ann Summers' shops of the seventies. I even tried to give them to the old 'rag and bone' man but instead of giving me a whistle, he dived for cover because he thought that I was a frigging Nazi. I gave him the two fingered salute and I put my 'mountain of Virginia' efforts on some old bonfire!...............................Bye Ollie!

Most of our clobber was bought in 'Jack Sharps or 'Gansgear' but if we were a bit skint then we would make do with 'Greaty' or the precinct in town. Many a bargain was bought in 'Greaty' market and worn with all the panache of a complete trend setter. I used to add my own few bob into the pot to make sure that I was literally making strides in this field by not wearing the tags that said "meff". Yes I had my pirate tee shirts and my white tennis pumps but I never had the indignity of having to wear a pair of 'Borstal runaways'. Only the Clampett's wore these ghastly trainers and they were a bit like 'Mitre Memphis' on steroids. My other fashion efforts at walking tall included my 'Moonbases' that were ankle boots and they were made out of light blue denim with a dead springy soul. You could walk like Neil Armstrong on the many craters of our parched land but I don't think that they were ever a giant step for 'all mankind'. Other fashion haunts on the agenda included 'Goldrush', 'Issy Crown', The Big 'S' and 'Patches'. My mother made sure that we were all turned out as bright as a button and sometimes she really did go without in order to get the three of us all the latest fads and trends. She looked upon us as her own dedicated followers of fashion and there were never any kinks in my clobber!

My very first pair of football boots also contrived to be a complete and utter disaster because I think that they were in fact made for rugby. I am sure that these torpedoes were constructed in Camel Laird by some 'arle' arse fellah who just had it in for me and my seemingly limited football endeavours. They were called 'Top dog' and I got them off our Gary I think because he had inherited his own pair of the higher ranking Adidas brand. I got into the school team but I reckon that they just felt sorry for me and I went on to be a great coat holder of my day. The only time I ever got picked for the team would be when it was freezing cold and no one could be bothered getting out of bed to turn up. I would knock for Gary McHarron and we would get on the 154 in Christian Street to Walton Hall Park where we would meet up with the rest of our crew. Our Franky was the real 'Roy' of our family but I did not mind at all because he was brilliant and I guess that he just got pushed a little bit more than me. I think our Lorraine was even better than me but I loved football anyway if just for the taking part. Taking part was the only aspect of my not so beautiful game but it did not stop me from playing at every opportunity and I was nowhere near as bad as I have made out. I said at the beginning of my book that it would be a little bit exaggerated and I was right because I was in fact an excellent footballer. I scored on and off the pitch and could have signed for Everton or Accrington Stanley but I had a paper round and that was very time consuming.

Halloween was always a great time for me too and I fondly remember running home from school to the old library on Christian Street. This was in order to get my ticket for the mission that was to be my little shop of horrors and all things nasty that go bump in the night. The scene did not need to be set because we were living on that massive graveyard so it was just adding the finer details like spiders and fangs or a phial of fake blood from the joke shop on Dale Street. There were ghouls everywhere and some of them could not help looking like ghouls so it was a night off for them I suppose. They staggered from pub to pub like something out of the thriller video but without the choreographed steps of course. Their dance moves were just made up as they went about their own business until the obligatory skit names would commence and eerily echo out in to the night sky. We would get chased everywhere and ultimately we would lead them into a trap that would have been set up hours before by Joey Roan or his sidekicks Gerry O' Rourke and Peter Sallery.

The square was full of pranksters and some of them were no bigger than myself (big Nora for instance!) We learned the ropes from the older lads and I perfected my skills to put my own twist on any proceedings that would involve comic capers or worse. The 'freaks' on the 'Vicky' were also in their element because it was the only night of the year that they blended in with everyone else. They inadvertently joined in and the scene was perfectly set for the proceedings that were taking place. This most garish of nights was played out by everyone in the vicinity and would always be one to remember in our calendar year. We included everyone at some point or other but them freaks were weird and definitely made for Halloween.

There were loads of weird people dotted about in our square but they were few and far between and then there was the downright scary. You would not want to bump into 'Mushy Nellie' on a dark night or 'Annie eyeball' for that matter because you really would have shit yourself. I would always do a double take whenever I saw these ghouls and I would be really shocked to see that these scary people were not even wearing masks. The 'Vicky' was always a back drop for strange goings on and it would often involve a penny peep show (don't ask) or something else that would be frowned upon today but I never took part in any of these unusual charades. The usual duck apple scenes would be commonplace on the many decorated doorsteps and it's sad to see that these old traditions have now somewhat diminished. I always remember nearly breaking my tooth on a tanner that was lodged inside one of these cider makers and that put me off duck apple for life. We would also put apples on a string and cover them in jam and then attempt to eat them with our hands behind our backs.

The jam would get everywhere and you would have to eat all of the apples that were left dangling to avoid tooth decay from the masses of sugar that we ingested. I reckon that every dentist in Liverpool dreaded Halloween because if the sugar did not wreck your teeth then the hidden tanners would. Some kids did not need the false fangs from the 'Ace place' on this spooky night because they had a perfect set of their own and hardly any make up was required either! Halloween gave way to bonfire night which I have already been through so I will now move on to Christmas time!

Seasonal greetings were always great for the Parry clan because there would always be a party to look forward to. We spent a lot of time together and many great memories were born in and around the whole of Liverpool. We would travel all over the city to share in the festivities with all of our relatives and the yuletide fun was never far away. Marie and Georgie Christians would always be a hoot because they both played the perfect hosts along with the box of toys. I spent many hours in their home and New Year's Eve would always be a very special occasion because we were allowed a little tipple. Georgie was an absolute gentleman to all of us and also a very funny man indeed who I will always remember with great respect. Him and Marie were a double act and they would always put us kids first because that's what our family was all about. My cousins Stephen and Tony had loads of boss toys and I always remember one Christmas night when I took all of the skin off my thumbs by playing 'Crossfire' for hours and hours on end.

Great days, but it was always the same with my over generous family and I thank them all for that. John and Sheila's home was forever blessed with good times and I had many wonderful times there with our David and the rest of the happy crew. One such occasion involved me getting drunk one Christmas night and turning into every one of the fab four Beatles. I sang every single song of note and played every imaginary instrument that was going until I fell over my invisible drums. Being 'half cut' did not help my situation but we always did have a riotous time and it was all done in the best possible taste. Sheila was a brilliant woman because she really did look after me when I was an elf and John was just a top uncle! Scrooge was nowhere to be seen in our own version of 'A Christmas Carol' because minge bags were not tolerated at this time of cheer. My overflowing pockets would be merrily jingling with masses of 'ten bob' pieces and the ghost of Christmas past was always very spirited!

My nana Parry's would always be full to the brim because her house was the focal point of every Christmas day. She would make me laugh with her pinafores and her bowl of peeled spuds that were an ever present feature in her hall. We would routinely bump into my aunty Pauline and Jim Mann who lived in Canada for a while until they saw the light and came back home to our shores. We were at Pauline's a lot and it was always an added pleasure when Mr. Mann (Jim's dad) was visiting them from bonny Scotland because he was class. I often babysat for Jim and Pauline and I would always take care of our Stephen and of course our sweet Caroline. I also visited my aunty Eileen and Sid Laing's on a number of frost bitten occasions and I think that it was definitely Eileen's kids and my cousins who got me into the mod movement. I loved their taste in music and I was a big fan of their 'rude boy' clobber which I tried to emulate but I just kept it simple because I was cool anyway. I opted for pink 'Ben Sherman's' and suede brogues that were both very liberating in my modern world of 'two tone' mania. Sid had a boss car and it was a gleaming Talbot Sunbeam which was so sporty and a real babe magnet in its day. He had a very dry wit which would often leave people in stitches with just his delivery on words and he was a very decent man. I can always remember Sid and my dad spraying the car bright yellow and this just added to the car's apparent appeal. Eileen and the rest of the clan shared many great festive times with us but my favourite memories would consist of playing football with our Phillip and Terry. Me and our kid would always give them a lesson in football but I am sure that they will be screaming at this book, "no way mate"! Come on lads the game is up because we learned our graceful moves on the vast beaches of Gerard Gardens!

The bleak mid-winter was so apparent and the snow would fall in abundance of crystals that would shimmer as they passed the masses of fairy lit windows. Sarah's would be chocker block and I always remember sweating cobs because of the intense heat of my budgie jacket. There would never be anywhere to sit down because the flat was so small but we all managed to get in somehow and it was a bit like musical chairs sometimes! Everyone would clamber for a seat next to my uncles Jimmy and Denis who would normally be feasting on Sarah's liver and onions underneath a picture of the Pope. Jimmy was a Labour councillor and also a great boxer of note whenever he donned those famous oven gloves in our back kitchen. We had many laughs on our vote grabbing days with Jimmy and the rest of the crew including my uncle Robbie who was of course a Member of Parliament. I shared millions of great memories with Robbie and his lovely wife Marie Heston and I appreciated everything that they had ever bestowed on me as a child. Marie used to always take us to the grotto in Lewis's and Christmas time would never be the same without her presence. Denis went on to be a priest and I hope that he has forgiven me for borrowing "sunny afternoon" by the Kinks off him and not returning it. Sorry Denis but I needed it for my singles collection and you can have it back as part of my ongoing penance.

There was an angelic picture on the wall of our Stephen that was next to 'Joey' the resident budgie's cage. He was a very pretty boy indeed and I do not mean our Stephen by the way although he would tell you otherwise. Joey was a legend and I remember crying my eyes out when he was found as dead as a parrot in a toilet roll by my grandad. My grandfather was a lovely man and I regarded him as an all time great because he would enlighten me with his own days of misspent youth. He would also inspire me on to better things and I can safely say that he was one of the finest men that I have ever met in my entire life. He was so genuine and always had lots of time for all of the kids who would descend on his and Sarah's home. Our Terry and

Joan also lived on the same landing as my nana Parry and again they were also a massive part of any celebrations that would be going on all around me. The rest of the crew I have already mentioned so stop being greedy and get on with the book will you!

All the Shields's crew were pretty local with the exception of our Willie and my aunty Joan who lived in the leafy suburbs of Maghull (great in the summer) and Kirkby (great for a kiss) respectively. Also my uncle Joey who lived in Peterborough but who we would see quite regularly and he was a very generous man as they all were. Poor Joey sadly died on one of the legendary mad Mondays and I guess that he would not have had it any other way. He would always leave his blue Ford 'prefect' on the 'ollar' and take the short but now fated walk past Gianelli's and into the Swan public house. They would all meet up on London Road and were joined by the rest of the 'motley crew' who made these Mondays so famous. My uncles who were part of this drinking legion were John, Willie, Mike, Vinnie and Danny. John who was married to Agnes lived with my other cousins on the East Lancashire Road but he too would also spend a lot of time in my nana's along with the rest of the clan. He was also great company and a very down to earth kind of geezer who I spent a lot of time with in my senior school years at Campion. I did not see much of my older cousins but I loved them just the same and they will always be a part of me. Vinnie Murphy and my aunty Marie lived up by the brow and Vinnie 'the gent' was my best mate because I would spend many a dinner hour with him. I would be able to stick down on my dinner money because they would always treat me to spaghetti on toast and biscuits while we listened to Mrs Butler's eldest on Radio City! Marie was lovely and she used to tell me off a lot but it was done out of love and I loved being in their company with biscuits and freshly brewed tea!

My favourite place to congregate though was my nana Shields's where our Teresa, Lily, Marie and Joan would often meet up with my mum and the jangling would begin at a very steady and rip roaring tempo. My nana would chair the debates like 'Judge Pickles' and I would just sit back in awe of these great women who I truly admired and still do with an underlying passion. Our Mike would just puff and blow with his quiff like a burst couch and he would have me off all the time for a chip butty or was that our John? John was very funny in his own dry way and you had to know him to get his gist because he was always very quick on the draw. He mastered the art of sarcasm but it was never ever spoken in a cynical way because his motives would always be quite the opposite and he continues to make me laugh to this day. John is also a great story teller and you can't help but laugh when he recounts all of his and my mother's childhood memories. My nana was an all round entertainer and she coined the phrases "Boily nosed bastard" and "kitty in the fridge" for anyone who dared to root in her fridge or any other places that would be deemed as out of bounds. We often called her 'Nellie pledge' which was only ever used in a loving way of course but I guess that she did not like that particular pseudonym for whatever reason. Teresa worked in 'Crawfords' biscuit factory so dinner time would always be a binge of 'mint bandits' and 'fruit clubs' for me and I always made sure that I visited her and Ronnie in Cantril Farm. I would come home with a big bag full of brokies and I would duly stash the lot under my bed!

My uncle Ronnie was the clown prince of his day and one of the funniest men that I ever had the pleasure of knowing as he paraded around in his crazy but very funny disguises. Young Ronnie would enthral me with his amazing adventures as a real life tin soldier and he was always very interesting because he would tell me all about his own dreams and aspirations. He was a real life 'Biggles' who went on to master the art of combat and his dreams turned into reality. As for our poor Karen, God bless her, she had the indignity of being the spitting image of me but we were both cute so we got over it and relished the complimentary teasing to some extent. We were also levelled with the same name of 'fingers Magill' by Nellie for our constant rooting exploits in the many bags that would be littered around the floor. It was always great going up to the farm because it was pure entertainment with the forever bungling Teresa who would create her own version of 'Carry on camping' while our Joanne and the rest of the audience would collapse in fits of laughter. Joanne got up to lots of mischief with me and our favourite form of mischief was 'knock and run' in the Crescent. Maghull was never dull either and our Gary would show me the delights of this very posh setting which in itself was a great adventure. I quickly acquired a subtle taste for the countryside and hastily moved on to their next door neighbour's apple trees! Joan and Charlie were always great hosts and I spent many a moon up there with our Gary tormenting our little Charlie and Jacqueline.

I must move back to Christmas time again now as I thank all of my cousins who are vast in their many numbers and who all contributed so much in me having such a wicked time. Thank you all so sincerely for giving me the great memories to keep forever that helped to shape some of my great moments of childhood and beyond. Christmas remained my best and happiest times of the year because it meant more family parties and of course everything that it would bring with it. The fairy lights would illuminate the cosy landings and added to the magic aura that was so apparent everywhere in this real life Santa's grotto. My dad used to be a wholesaler so we had access to all of the best toys like 'Ker-Plunk' and 'Etch a sketch' and we would not really have to root to see what we had because we got loads anyway. Still it did not stop us from mooching and one night I got my fingers burned big time as I would foolishly assume that anything that was stashed in the back bedroom was in fact mine. I was 'kittying' again and I found a top of the range skateboard on top of my dad's wardrobe. It was hidden underneath a jigsaw puzzle of the Niagara Falls and lots of other clutter but I spotted its gleaming wheels and excitedly pulled it down. I was convinced that it was one of my presents so I took it for a test run on the landing and just as I did a 'catarmaran' I saw me arle fellah doing a 'tic tac' up the stairs and he well and truly nicked me. I was given a right telling off and not for being out late but for the fact that the skateboard was not even mine but one of the other kids in the square. It had been paid for on the drip by his ma and now I had some real explaining to do. I had to clean the wheels up with some 'Mr. Sheene' and 'Duraglit' and even had to drop it off the next morning but I walked away from my Father Christmas role with a tanner and a very sheepish smile on my face. Another classic Christmas carol was when we got up early on Christmas morning and as our way of saying thanks for our presents we decided to ignite the lovely coal fire. Anyway we put all of the ashes into the Liverpool echo and whoooooosh!.....! The frigging lot went up and burned a hole right through the paper and on to the newly carpeted floor. We spent most of Christmas day singing silent night to each other but we were soon to be forgiven as we feasted on our Curly Wurlys and a helping of the Morecambe and Wise show for afters. It really did seem that everything I touched would turn into gold and this just continued to happen throughout the years. It added to the self-proclaimed notion that I was in fact truly blessed in my quest to become minted. I was living in this kaleidoscope of dreams that were taking place within my mind and more so in my heart of hearts!

Other great seasonal memories included my gorgeous aunty Peggy Ryan and her lovely husband Hughie always being around at Christmas time. We would all get a selection box each and a *Topper* annual or something else that would always be beautifully presented and wrapped accordingly. Their sons Joseph and Nicholas would also be on the scene and I remember our Joseph bought me a Wacky Races annual that I treasured and I still remind him of it every time we speak. Joseph went on to be a priest and I was deeply honoured to have him and my uncle Denis who is also a priest oversee and who blessed my mother's funeral in April 2010. Just like her, the funeral was lovely and was conducted so beautifully and intimately by my very own clan to whom I am eternally grateful to forever! Our Nicholas also fits into the fray because he was responsible for eating a full box of cakes to himself whilst he was babysitting for us. The holiday period would always involve indulgence and he blamed us for his binge but he definitely will not forget about this one now will he? Revenge on you oh un-saintly Nicholas and served upon you a lot sweeter than the cakes that you scoffed down on that not so holy of nights. As usual all of my aunties and uncles would open their homes for us and together they gave us the true spirit of Christmas and a mind so chocker block with good memories. I cannot get all of them out because it would take too long and I would have to write about another 200 pages at least. All the same I would like to offer a massive thank you to everyone who participated in these good if not great happy tidings.

The best part though would be waking up at about four in the morning and creeping into the kitchen to see what Father Christmas had brought us. After stepping over my uncle Jimmy Joyce or the legendary Joe Joyce I would make my way over to my pile of presents by the veranda. These two great uncles were both ace and always gave us more than a couple of bob every time they saw us and it always seemed to be around Christmas time. The see through wrapping paper would be off in seconds flat as I would feast my eyes on maybe an Atari console or an electric organ that was to be the inspiration of our many ghost night stories with my uncle Willie. He sat and played like a latter day Doctor Phibes as he hammered down on to the under siege keys in E minor. My cousins in Kirkby must have had a ball with Willie on the family stage because he really was one of the great entertainers in life and he was an absolute legend to all who knew him. My aunty Hannah went on to be my biggest fan and would often kick off on Billy Butler for not playing my dodgy songs on the radio but here I am now girl and finally I'm nearly famous. You and me mum can jib that Paul Potts fellah now because hopefully the time is right for me to actually shine and that is just 'custy' in my book of innocent accolades. Finally and on to what was to become my best ever present as a kid and one that I found a companion in for life who was of course Dick Redhead. He was my crash test dummy that went with me everywhere when I was just a bin lid and he was probably the most loyal friend that I ever had. He was a real character who was to be my guy on bommie night and my trusted lieutenant on my many other adventures. Dick would literally come alive with his own personality and take over from where I left off to captivate everyone who happened to be in our company. I don't know what happened to poor old Dick but I think he went on to have a great grandchild called Chucky who himself was a drummer in the Orange Lodge and the rest is history as they say!

The cold winters did not seem to register with me and my only reminder of this barren time was my snorkel and frostbitten hands in front of the coal fire. I used to make my own ice cream with milk and snow but the sherbet was often replaced by gravel and the flake would probably be a present off Rocky Parry! Rocky was a loveable mutt who went on to be the first Rastafarian in Gerard Crescent because he had dreadlocks on his bitty arse. He would get everywhere and was my nana's loyal companion for many years until he died whilst smoking a bong in Cazeneau Street. We built fires all of the time in the square and with the floodlights being on when darkness fell, it made this scenery so intimate and warm in its own blissful splendour. All of my great memories were played out in this tropical aquarium and we were the school of fish that flourished in its happy waters. We lived inside this pool of life and did not need any outside influences whatsoever because we were so happy with our own lot. People never really complained about anything other than the social issues that were felt by everyone from time to time and the obvious neglect of our giant fish tank. The happy aquarium was even painted on the wall in the gardens itself as we attempted one final makeover of this failing kingdom but it really was too little too late. These little fish were small fries and they were being quickly gobbled up by the sharks who were dressed to kill in their pin stripe suits. I was drowning in grief and I swam to the safety of dry land that was surrounded by trees but I would always long to be back where I was born!

Yes the older lads had robbed cars and yes we were dubbed "The violent playground" but give me any other community in the world that was so salt of the earth and caring. I will give anyone who replies a pile of rocking horse shit in return and I will guarantee you that a better class of people will never ever be found anywhere else on this planet. The minority of mindless knockers who try to give us a bad name are only jealous because they probably did not even belong here and only became tenants in the 1980s. The picture that I have painted in this book was my Gerard Gardens and nobody else's until

I decided to finally put it into print. Maybe I should deem this book more fittingly as a mini autobiography that started in 1967 and finishes with utter dread in 1978. During that immortal year my world came crashing down on me forever as I fell apart when it was announced that we were actually leaving the square! Not even 'Archie' the 'cocky watchman' could save us from our impending fall from grace and everything that was done to try and save this art deco palace was sadly done in vain. Mates like Joey and Billy Maddox had not long moved into the squares and here I was saying goodbye to them already. I had formed many good bonds in Gerard Gardens and I was now very sad and despondent to be finally letting go of my many friends and more importantly my safe sanctuary!

Every other part of the year would see us through the seldom dark days and yes there were a few but the sun would always rise up from the crescent to replenish our happy status. It was a scene that would inspire any kid in the area to get up, get dressed and get into the square that was our own theatre of dreams. This great complex was like a never ending Disney animation but the planners had other ideas and the dream went horribly wrong. The dreams of children were interwoven into a nightmare of titanic proportions as the gargoyles of Westminster harboured their motives to finally prevail. These smiling assassins from another planet behaved like bastard apes as they put our landscape under attack and left our beautiful gardens to rot. People gathered around to talk about the imminent danger that was now so apparent and we all quickly realised that the planet that we had lived on for many years was about to be taken over by greedy developers. The old fruit and veg barrow in the arches disappeared as 'Bridie' said goodbye amongst other institutions and people congregated in the square to pour out their feelings. This threat was very real and it was now hanging over our heads like some kind of unwanted lead balloon. The death knell ominously sounded out with a very loud and very clear message that our tenure was coming to a depressing end. Unfortunately, no one was listening and it was not long before all of the talk became fact and the curtain finally closed on this unique empire state forever!

Well I think that I have covered everything now as my journey begins to wind down and I take the final steps of finishing my fairy tale. The only things that I may have missed out were my girlfriends of the time but there were only a few and one particular girl who was double my age but who I had a massive crush on. Rita Mcharron was my mate Gary's sister and she was stunning but so out of my league because she was older than me and to her I was just a little chipmunk. Anyway, this 'Mork' would never get his 'Mindy' and I really did try so hard but I always ended up hitting a brick wall. I would walk her up her mates every night in Soho Street and I would have done anything for her because I was so smitten. I even snided off from my mate Brian Duncan on the odd occasion but it was well worth it because all of my mates were very jealous of my imaginary girlfriend. She broke my heart when she announced that she was moving to Germany and them bastard Nazis done my head in once again. We kept in touch via air mail and by a red telephone box that took my two pence pieces by the bucket full as I spoke to her for ages and ages nearly every night. I would always get my pennies back though with the help of a lolly ice stick and a half eaten bubbly but she was never to be my real girlfriend and that put me off relationships for life.

Other girlfriends were nothing more than a quick fumble in a skip or maybe a proper neck in the subways if I would be so lucky. We used these skips as 'love shacks' and they would also be great for dangling from when they were lifted on to the backs of the wagons. I was a bit of a stud really but in a very innocent way and yes I would chase lots of girls who in turn would chase me. Often enough it would be for all the wrong reasons and I would never learn my lessons in love until it was way too late. I remember Jane Shea practically ripping my quiff off my scalp in the 'backie' for reasons unknown to me and Jane in her defence reckons that it was definitely Catherine Fay. I will forever wonder who the real culprit actually was and I hold them both responsible for me now being as bald as a coot. Me and Jenko were always being chased out of houses that the girls would be baby sitting in but it never stopped us from being part of the rat pack that the girls would seemingly love us for. Annmarie Welch was my chick and I think that Paul was just with anyone who would jump into a skip with him and relieve him of his red and black snake belt which he wore so menacingly. I always fancied Stella Melia but I think that the fact that I had grassed on our Lorraine over the crisps caper put her off and I was always too scared to ask her just in case she slapped my face. Finally on to the girl who was the girl of my dreams but who was that gorgeous that I used to just look at her and go bright red in infatuation. Maria Muscatelli was definitely my 'Little Italy' and I told her so many years later as we both laughed and relived our great days of unspoiled romance. These romantic interludes were being played out in every corner of the square and I fitted in to all four corners at one time or another. Thanks girls for keeping my blue blood red and for giving me just as much excitement as the many other friends that I made along the many paths of my reminiscent past!

I am now running out of steam and I feel as though that I have just got to mention the Golden Jubilee of 1977 before we go our separate ways. This was the best party of the best year that I have ever lived in and I suppose that it was something of a swan song for me. It was also the year that I had the chicken pox and thousands of 'Jocks' descended on us as Scotland were playing at Anfield in a world cup qualifier with Wales. The Scottish fans were a real sight to be seen and to me it was just like a massive Bay City rollers gig that was being played out in our hospitable gardens. The tartan army lapped it up and probably could not believe just how welcoming the residents really were and I will bet you a haggis to a packet of spangles that many of them still marvel about their exploits on this very special day.

The jubilee itself was great and it was to be my last orders as the final curtain fell down on my eleven magical years as a happy resident. I had definitely made my mark as a native but more so as a character of this comic fabled hunting ground and I was sure that I would be remembered. We all got a Jubilee 'flyaway' ball which we would kick on to the top landings and we also received a collectable coin that was instantly exchanged for a cap gun with loads of caps on a little red roll. The party lasted all day in the glare of red, white and blue bunting that displayed the colours of both our beloved teams so it added to the notion that we were all indeed very much as one. All of the mothers spent months planning this big extravaganza and all of their efforts definitely paid off in many more ways than one. It was to be our last big party together and when all of the bunting had disappeared the stark reality was one of not so colourful proportions. The party for me was over forever and now I had to also say goodbye to all of the meaningful things that were so good and bad about this great place that I had loved so much!

The lights went out for me in 1978 and I left these magical gardens with my head well and truly up my arse as I faced the harsh reality of not being a 'Gardenite' anymore! I trudged down the stairs for the last time and I took in a massive deep breath and thus taking the garden air in with me as I whispered goodbye. I left my heart there forever and all of my mates too, along with all of the characters that I have mentioned in this monopoly of laughs that I contrived to put together. I sincerely hope that I have not offended anyone at all in this book including the Orange Lodge folk and the four squares because without them I could not have completed my mission so I thank you all. As I have stressed throughout this book, my fables are all seen through the eyes of a child and at the time it was happening for real inside my mind. I must also say that the above mentioned are also a solid crew and are very decent people themselves who I both embrace and thank for giving me so many good memories to look back on. The Orange Lodge put on a good show and I have many friends who are protestant so times really have moved on in that sense. It's a bit like football I suppose or even Marmite but I admire all of my counterparts just the same and I hope that I have made them all laugh. My heart will never wander anywhere else in the world because anywhere else just does not matter to me so I am happy to leave it in such a restful place.

It just remains to be said a massive thank you to you all and way too many to mention all at once but you all know who you are. I hope my book is seen by everyone who shared these great times with me and for the people who I have not mentioned I really am sorry especially to all of my cousins. Every single one of you has flashed some kind of inspiration in and out of my mind at some stage and you are all definitely in this book in one way or another. Please read this book to your children and make sure that you fill in any bits that I may have missed out or boyishly glossed over in my intolerable excitement. My final thoughts on this great voyage will end for now but the dream will surely live on in each and every one of you forever. Anyone who I have ever 'had over' in life can now get me back by just getting this book for free out of the library or by just borrowing it off someone else who has already bought it. If you are one of these people then we are quits now and the rest of yiz will just after wait until I have sold enough copies of this book!

My departure from the squares has got to go down as the worst ever time in my life up to that point and one that I would never fully recover from. I tasted insecurity for the very first time in my life and felt pain on a scale that I did not even know existed. The terrifying prospect of leaving the squares overwhelmed me but I still harboured the hope that one day I would return to this land of giants and once again prosper there with my own kids. Never once did I think that this colossus of a place would ever get demolished but like all of the nightmares that had gone before me this one was definitely real. I still shudder at the thought of what these bastard powers that be ultimately enforced upon us and I will never forgive these morons for as long as I live.

After the great summer of 1977 that brought us droughts and jubilees I was saying goodbye to the only world that I had ever known. The one place that had made me so happy for so long was being ripped away from me and right before my very own disbelieving eyes. I walked away forever in 1978 and I could only go back there as a visitor but it was never the same for me anymore because I felt like an outsider. This is where my journey now ends because sadly I cannot write any more about the years that finally led to its demise and its final days of demolition. In 1986 Gerard Gardens was demolished and I was not there but my heart was and always will be. I am forever haunted by the scenes of desecration and the ethnic cleansing that followed in a path that would ultimately lead to the ruination of a monument so sacred and blessed. Poor Lenny Boffey tried one last act of rebellion but it was all in vain because there was no way back from this horror show. We were well and truly shafted by these bigoted people and this now leads me to just say goodbye to you all. Farewell from me folks and I hope that I see you all at the book launch. This will be another great night and it will be like a reunion for us all to come together again for our final fling of sorts. My love and gratitude to you all!

Gerard Gardens poem and song by Bobby Parry!

What I wouldn't give to go back to the days,
of playing in the square that now seems like a haze.
Underneath the floodlight's, playing kick the can,
talking with the neighbours, rob the mobile van!

There's Maggie wailing down the stairs, shouting at the kids, knockers going usual things, rob the dustbin lids.
You had four walls and an arch, standing proudly there,
in came labour who shipped us out, to desecrate our square!

Gerard, where have you gone? l long to see your smile.
The men who made the wrong decisions, should be sent for trial!
You were my home security, just give me the key,
I'll climb the stairs ain't got no lift, to number 7b.

Now you've gone without a trace, I'm left with memories,
to the ground you were razed, like gardens without trees.

Standing on the landing, mums give kids a pound,
talking with the neighbours, feeling safe and sound!

Peeping Tom, kick the can, Mary kill the cat,
people I remember, from days spent in my flat.
Doors are left wide open, an element of trust,
Grandma's on the veranda, feed the birds a crust!

Gerard, where have you gone? Why did they destruct?
Replace your splendour with estates, to me, they look half cooked.
Far too young to make a point, of having you reprieved,
at least I'm left with memories, for that I am relieved!

Goodbye Gerard, rest in peace, time to move along,
Jubilees and teddy boys, now sing a different song.
Hit the post, knock and run, now seems worlds apart,
I'm picking up the pieces, goodbye horse and cart...GOODBYE!

(Copyright Bobby Parry!)

Just to prove that my allegiance to the crescent is always present I submit this anecdote for you all!

"I SAW THE CRESCENT IN MY GARDENS OF EDEN"

Copyright Bobby Parry (27th July 2010)

My Thanks...

On completion of this book, I am happy to say that I finally got my hands on one of the famous dummies that featured throughout this book. I got Dick Redhead on ebay for £50 and it really was a bargain to be had. He was in a sorry state but with the help of my seamstress "Patricia the zipper" he has now been restored to his former glory. Thanks Pat for doing a great job with Dick's suit and he has asked me to pass on his kind regards.

Special thanks to my cousin Charles Pepper who will be the master of ceremonies on my book launch and also to the band "The Gardens" for supporting me on this very special night of celebration! The night in question will be held in the Liner Hotel which is situated in Lord Nelson Street and this book is your free ticket in. I have subsidised this book and the launch night myself, and my only aim is to break even which reflects in the price of this publication. Thank you all from the bottom of my pencil case!

I would also like to dedicate this book to John Emmerson who sadly passed away in the process of my book being published. John was the founder of Countyvise and I sincerely hope that my work has done this very fine man proud. Special thanks also to everyone at Countyvise and especially to Cathy Hunter, Charles McIntyre and of course Mrs Emmerson!

Special thanks to the following people for your much appreciated support throughout my incredible journey; Franky Parry, Charles Pepper, Gerard Fleming, Joseph O 'Connell, The "Gardens band", Annmarie Welch, Michael Tallon, Paul Birchall, Paul Jenkins, Francis Carlyle, Paul Nicholson, Christine Hanratty, Lesley Russell, and every one of my family and friends who have really encouraged me to get my mini autobiography published!